Quality in Child Care: What Does Research Tell Us?

Ministry of Education, Ontario
Information Centre, 13th Floor,
Mowat Block, Queen's Park,
Toronto. Ont.   M7A 1L2

RESEARCH MONOGRAPHS OF THE NATIONAL ASSOCIATION
FOR THE EDUCATION OF YOUNG CHILDREN, VOLUME 1

Quality in Child Care: What Does Research Tell Us?

Deborah A. Phillips, Editor

A 1986–87 Comprehensive Membership Benefit

National Association for the Education of Young Children
Washington, D.C.

Photo credits: Subjects & Predicates *16, 60, 80;* © B. Schafer *20;* Nancy P. Alexander *42;* © 1987 Bruce Jennings *101;* © Cleo Freelance Photo *107.*

Copyright © 1987 by Deborah A. Phillips. All rights reserved.

Copyright © 1987 for Chapter 2, "Predicting Child Development From Child Care Forms and Features: The Chicago Study," and Chapter 7, "In Search of Consistencies in Child Care Research," is held by K. Alison Clarke-Stewart.

National Association for the Education of Young Children
1834 Connecticut Avenue, N.W.
Washington, DC 20009-5786

Library of Congress Catalog Card Number: 87-062195

ISBN Catalog Number: 0-935989-08-0

NAEYC #140

PRINTED IN THE UNITED STATES OF AMERICA.

*This monograph is dedicated to
Edward Zigler,
who inspired my commitment to
high quality child care*

Contents

	PAGE
Preface	ix

Chapter 1   **1**
Indicators of Quality in Child Care: Review of Research
    Deborah A. Phillips and Carollee Howes

Chapter 2   **21**
Predicting Child Development From Child Care Forms and Features: The Chicago Study
    K. Alison Clarke-Stewart

Chapter 3   **43**
Dimensions and Effects of Child Care Quality: The Bermuda Study
    Deborah A. Phillips, Sandra Scarr, and Kathleen McCartney

Chapter 4   **57**
Child Care Quality, Compliance with Regulations, and Children's Development: The Pennsylvania Study
    Susan Kontos and Richard Fiene

Chapter 5   **81**
Quality Indicators in Infant and Toddler Child Care: The Los Angeles Study
    Carollee Howes

Chapter 6   **89**
Effects of Child Care, Family, and Individual Characteristics on Children's Language Development: The Victoria Day Care Research Project
    Hillel Goelman and Alan Pence

Chapter 7   **105**
In Search of Consistencies in Child Care Research
    K. Alison Clarke-Stewart

Epilogue	121
Index	127
Contributors	131
Information About NAEYC	132

I would like to thank each of the anonymous reviewers for being so generous with their time and so creative with their comments on the chapters that comprise this monograph.

Preface

GOOD QUALITY IS seen by many as the luxury issue in child care. Pressures to expand the supply and depress the costs of child care have consistently shortchanged efforts to improve the quality of child care in the United States. Costs, rather than the well-being of children, have shaped our public policies about child care.

One must look to research to find systematic attention to questions of child care quality. Quality has, in fact, become the central topic of study among early educators and developmental psychologists. Having moved beyond obsolete debates about *whether* child care helps or harms development and about *which types* of child care are best, researchers are now asking, "*How* can we make child care better?" Accordingly, research is now beginning to capture the vast diversity among child care environments and to relate this diversity to how children fare in child care.

This monograph presents and summarizes this *third wave* of research — as characterized by Alison Clarke-Stewart in Chapter 7—on key indicators of child care quality. We ask: "Can we identify reliable components of good quality care?" "What are they?" "What is their relation to children's family environments?" We hope our preliminary answers can begin to guide the efforts of practitioners and spur action among policymakers to upgrade the quality of our nation's child care.

The authors who have contributed to the monograph are among the most prominent child care researchers. Alison Clarke-Stewart's Chicago Study of Child Care and Development stands alone as an example of research that encompasses both multiple forms (in-home care, family day care, child care centers, and nursery schools) and qualitative features of child care. Clarke-Stewart's study in this volume describes the quality of life for children in different child care arrangements and explores whether it is the type or the features of child care that determine the quality of the environment.

The research conducted by Sandra Scarr, Kathleen McCartney, and myself was instrumental in alerting the field to the necessity of incorporating differences in children's child care experience and family backgrounds when studying the effects of wide differences in child care quality on children's development. The results from our Bermuda Study, reported here, focus on the social development of children who attended child care centers that varied widely in quality. We also address timely issues concerning children's age of entry and length of time in child care as they interact with aspects of quality.

The Pennsylvania Day Care Study, conducted by Susan Kontos and

Richard Fiene, provides a model of policy research. This study was designed in collaboration with the child care licensing office in Pennsylvania, which sought to pinpoint the most critical aspects of child care quality as a means to target its monitoring efforts. The Kontos and Fiene chapter thus addresses the critical distinction between regulatable and nonregulatable indicators of child care quality. They also compare profit and nonprofit child care centers.

Carollee Howes has been among the first to venture into the controversial territory of infant and toddler child care. She has also added a new aspect of good quality to the debate, namely, the stability of the caregivers. Her chapter in this volume examines the dimensions of caregiver stability and training, and staff-child ratios in centers that serve infants and toddlers.

Hillel Goelman and Alan Pence also entered uncharted waters by including a sample of unlicensed family day care homes, along with licensed homes and centers, in their Victoria Day Care Research Project in Canada. The Victoria Study is also quite unique in its reliance on highly detailed observations of children's spontaneous play in child care as a process measure of quality. In this volume, Goelman and Pence focus on children's language development in child care.

These five research chapters are bounded by a summary of the research evidence on indicators of child care quality and by Alison Clarke-Stewart's comparison and synthesis of these new research results.

The research reported in this volume reflects the full range of quality that is available to most parents who need child care. Unlike much of the research of the last two decades, this new crop of results is not restricted to examining a narrow range of high quality care. Instead, these studies exemplify the importance of considering low quality child care environments, as well as high, if indicators and effects of quality — as experienced by children — are to be identified.

Each of these studies also places questions of child care quality in the context of children's families. Parents select their children's child care environments, thus posing a challenge to researchers who seek to attribute child outcomes to the quality of these environments, rather than to family factors that may lead certain types of parants to select better or worse child care arrangements. Moreover, developmental outcomes for children are bound to derive from both their home *and* child care environments. The authors whose research is reported here have each included measures of children's home environments in an attempt to capture the interdependence of children's child care and family settings.

These studies are also unique in their reliance on labor-intensive, but essential, "eyes on" measures of child care quality. Type of care was not used, as it has been, as a proxy for quality. Anecdotal reports of parent satisfaction were not presumed to measure the actual quality of the care provided. Each research design involved extensive observations and interviews to obtain firsthand data on child care quality.

By 1995, two-thirds of all children younger than age 6 and three-quarters of school-age children are projected to have working mothers.* Childrearing, in practice, has become a collaborative endeavor. This means that growing numbers of children are spending larger portions of their young lives in child care. As a society, we can no longer ignore questions about the quality of their child care environments.

The first step is to identify some of the enduring ingredients of good quality. Only then can practitioners and policymakers put this knowledge into action. This volume is an attempt to provide some initial insights into this issue from state-of-the-art research. We are still far from generating a short list of key ingredients, and this may, in fact, be an impossible goal. But, together, the contributions to this monograph illustrate the means and the value of pursuing answers to the question "What is high quality child care?" if we are ever to make this goal a reality for children.

Deborah A. Phillips
University of Virginia

---

* Hofferth, S.L., & Phillips, D.A. (1987). Child care in the United States, 1970 to 1995. *Journal of Marriage and the Family, 49*(3) 559–571.

Chapter 1

Indicators of Quality Child Care: Review of Research

Deborah A. Phillips and Carollee Howes

As OF 1986, the majority of children younger than age 6, including more than half of those younger than 1 year of age, were in need of child care while their mothers worked. This demographic fact had a profound effect on the major issues addressed in child care research. The question of whether or not children should be in child care has become obsolete. We have also been able to move beyond this question because 20 years of research on child care allayed our worst fears that nonmaternal care was inevitably harmful to children. To the contrary, the overwhelming message was that children in good quality child care show no signs of harm, and children from low-income families may actually show improved cognitive development (Clarke-Stewart & Fein, 1983; Rutter, 1981; Zigler & Gordon, 1982).

The key to this basic conclusion lies in the term *good quality*. Most of the supporting research involved high quality, often university-based child care centers, which are not representative of the child care options available to most parents. Just as homes vary in the experiences they afford children, so do child care arrangements. Accordingly, researchers moved on to capture this diversity.

The National Day Care Study

The National Day Care Study launched this next phase of empirical research (Ruopp, Travers, Glantz, & Coelen, 1979). The federal government initiated the study to guide the construction of national child care standards. The task was to identify key provisions that best predict good outcomes for children and to develop cost estimates for offering these provisions.

The major results both contradicted and confirmed the intuitive wisdom of the field. Staff-child ratios, long heralded as a significant quality indicator, contributed only minimally to developmental effects for preschoolers in center-based care. Group size and specialized caregiver training emerged as the most potent predictors of positive classroom dynamics and child outcomes. In classrooms with smaller groups, lead teachers engaged in more social interaction with children; children were more cooperative, innovative and involved in tasks, and talkative; and children made greater gains on cognitive tests. Lead teachers with child-related education spent more time in social interaction with the children; the children in their classes showed more cooperation and greater task persistence; and, in centers with higher proportions of trained caregivers, preschoolers made greater cognitive test score gains.

Additionally, preschoolers made more rapid gains on cognitive tests in centers whose staff and directors voiced concern about cognitive development and emphasized individual development rather than group experiences. The investigators interpreted this finding as buttressing the hypothesis that cognitive outcomes in child care are particularly responsive to children's interactions with their caregivers, rather than with materials and other children.

The results of the National Day Care Study were a little different for center-based infant and toddler care. Both staff-child ratios and group size emerged as significant influences on caregiver behavior and child development. Infants in programs with fewer caregivers per child and larger groups showed more overt distress and apathy than infants in programs with high ratios and small groups. Low ratios were also associated, as were large groups, with increased staff time spent in management or control situations and less social interaction and cognitive/language stimulation with children.

So few of the infant caregivers had received specialized training that the effects of this factor could not be determined. However, overall years of education were positively related to the amount of social interaction and cognitive/language stimulation in toddler groups and to lower ratings of child apathy and potential danger in infant groups.

In sum, the National Day Care Study identified group size and specialized caregiver training as significant elements of child care quality in center-based programs for preschoolers and added staff-child ratios to these elements for infant and toddler care. This study also proposed that the association between these regulatable variables and children's development in child care is largely a function of their facilitating effect on caregivers' efforts to interact in positive, stimulating ways with the children in their care.

Contemporary research on child care quality

Has subsequent research confirmed these broad conclusions of the National Day Care Study, called them into question, or extended them to other settings, other elements of quality, or other outcomes? The answer to each of these questions is "yes." Since 1979, research that has attempted to reproduce the results of the National Day Care Study has confirmed some of the results, contradicted others, and forged new areas of inquiry.

During the last 10 years, researchers have increasingly acknowledged the complexity of defining quality in child care. In response, they have adopted multiple methods to assess quality, examined a wider range of child care arrangements, and placed these questions about quality in a broader context that considers the interdependence of child care and family environments.

Quality, by its nature, is a fuzzy concept. Nowhere is this felt more acutely than by parents who ask, "How can I know what's right for my child?" In research, quality has been viewed in several ways. First, global assessments of quality have been used to capture the overall climate of a program. Second, efforts to extract the specific dimensions of child care quality have emphasized (a) structural aspects of child care, such as group composition and staff qualifications, (b) dynamic aspects of child care that capture children's daily experiences, and (c) contextual aspects of child care, such as type of setting and staff stability. A third, and relatively new, perspective encompasses the joint effects of child care quality and children's family environments.

Global assessments of child care quality

Most observers of child care will readily acknowledge that good things go together. Vandell and Powers (1983), for example, found that high quality, university-run centers had high levels of teacher training, large amounts of space per child, and good staff-child ratios. This inevitable confounding of individual quality measures led some researchers to treat quality as a global construct.

Three approaches have been used. The first combined discrete indicators of quality into a composite measure by which programs are evaluated as either high or low in quality. Howes and Olenick (1986), for example, divided child care centers into high and low quality groups using as criteria for high quality (a) adult-child ratios no lower than 1:4 for children 2 years old or younger and 1:7 for children aged 30 months or older, (b) the presence of caregivers with formal training in child development, and (c) staff turnover that did not exceed two teachers per year. They found that toddlers in high quality centers were significantly more compliant in child care and were better able to resist the temptation to play with forbidden toys and to eat forbidden food in a laboratory session.

Using a similar method that relied on ratios, staff training, and space as quality criteria, Vandell and Powers (1983) found that children in high quality centers were more likely to engage in positive social interactions and behaviors than children enrolled in moderate and low quality centers, who displayed more solitary and unoccupied behavior.

A second approach to obtaining a global assessment of quality relies on a rating scale that taps multiple areas of program quality. Using observations of centers, the Early Childhood Environment Rating Scale, commonly called ECERS, (Harms & Clifford, 1980) leads to scores on seven dimensions of quality: (1) personal care, (2) creative activities, (3) language/reasoning activities, (4) furnishings/display, (5) fine/gross motor activities, (6) social development, and (7) adult facilities/opportunities. Summing scores across these seven dimensions generates an overall quality assessment.

This is the approach taken by the Bermuda Study (see Chapter 3). After the researchers eliminated the adult facilities subscale, the other six dimensions were found to be highly interrelated and were thus used to create a summary score. This score predicted children's intellectual, language, and social development, such that children in higher quality centers showed more advanced communication skills and verbal intelligence (McCartney, 1984) and more positive social behavior and task orientations (Phillips, McCartney, & Scarr, 1987).

Finally, important policy questions have been raised about whether good quality child care can achieve the effects that have been demonstrated for early childhood intervention programs. Efforts to answer these questions also require that programs be evaluated using global assessments of quality. The Bermuda data, for example, were reanalyzed to address the question of whether child care can serve as an effective intervention for low-income children (McCartney, Scarr, Phillips, & Grajek, 1985). One of the child care centers examined in Bermuda was substantially higher in quality than the other centers. It was run by the government and served primarily low-income families. In comparisons with both a subgroup of

Good quality child care can serve as an effective intervention for children from low-income families.

low-income children and the entire sample of children attending the nongovernment, lower quality centers, the low-income children attending the government-run center were found to have significantly better language skills and to be more considerate and sociable. Apparently good quality child care can serve as an effective intervention for children from low-income families (see also Ramey & Haskins, 1981).

In sum, global assessments of quality have confirmed common sense knowledge that better child care is better for children. This conclusion is not insignificant, however, in light of the telling qualification it places on questions of *whether* child care is detrimental, neutral, or beneficial for children's development. Without attention to the quality of the child care in which children spend their days, answers to the either/or question of sheer enrollment in child care are not only obsolete, but also uninformative.

Structural dimensions of quality

While it is true that good things co-occur in child care, global assessments of quality are of little use to practitioners and policymakers who seek to influence specific program features that predict positive outcomes for children. Moreover, some of the good things may have a more powerful impact on children's development than others.

These issues were addressed in research that examined specific structural dimensions of child care quality. The greatest attention has been paid to the dimensions identified by the National Day Care Study — adult-child ratio, group size, and caregiver training and experience. This review thus focuses on these dimensions.

Adult-child ratio. Ratio is considered an important quality indicator on the basis of assumptions that adult caregivers mediate children's contact with the social and physical world. Through social games, verbal interaction, and physical contact, caregivers offer children opportunities to practice and enjoy social exchanges, learn about the properties of objects, and acquire a sense of security and self-worth.

The number of children with whom each caregiver can engage in a stimulating and sensitive fashion is obviously limited. With too many children to care for, the caregiver's interactions with each child are likely to become brief and cursory. What does research tell us?

The majority of studies have found that the ratio has a significant effect on adult and child behavior in child care. Among the outcomes affected are the amount of adult-child imitation (Francis & Self, 1982), children's verbal interaction (Field, 1980; Howes & Rubenstein, 1985; Smith &

Staff-child ratios have a significant effect on adult and child behavior in child care.

Connolly, 1981), children's engagement in play (Bruner, 1980; Field, 1980; Howes & Rubenstein, 1985), and nurturant, nonrestrictive caregiver behavior (Howes, 1983; Howes & Rubenstein, 1985; Smith & Connolly, 1981). These results are from research studying infant and toddler as well as preschool-age child care in centers and family day care homes.

Group size. As with ratio, interest in group size derives from both developmental considerations about the critical socializing function of child care providers and practical considerations about the demands on caregivers' time. The results of the National Day Care Study also spurred interest in group size as a critical structural feature of child care.

The research evidence is quite clear. Smaller groups appear to facilitate constructive caregiver behavior and positive developmental outcomes for children. Howes (1983) found that larger groups were associated with less social stimulation and responsiveness in both center and family day care settings and more negative affect and restriction on the part of family day care providers. Howes and Rubenstein (1985) further found that children in small groups were more talkative. Stith and Davis (1984) studied family day care homes and also found that larger groups were associated with less positive affect and less responsiveness to infant distress on the part of caregivers.

In studies of center-based care, similar results emerge. Bruner (1980) viewed more pretend play and more elaborate play by children in smaller centers (fewer than 26 children). Similarly, Cummings and Beagles-Ross (1983) found that children in small centers (8 to 12 children) showed more positive affect and less avoidance upon entering their child care centers than children in larger centers (20 to 25 children).

Clarke-Stewart and Gruber (1984) present a more complex picture of the effects of group size. Consistent with the negative associations observed in other studies, children in family day care homes, centers, and classes with large enrollments were less sociable and cooperative with strangers, especially unfamiliar peers, than children in child care settings with small enrollments. But children in large classes were also more knowledgeable about the stranger's social perspective and less likely to behave negatively with the unfamiliar peer. Large enrollments may have positive as well as negative consequences.

Caregiver training, education, and experience. The skills and experience that child care providers bring to their jobs, as in any profession, are presumed to affect the quality of their performance. Accordingly, experience, education, and training are often used as indicators of caregiver competence. A central controversy in this area is whether

Smaller groups appear to facilitate constructive caregiver behavior and positive developmental outcomes for children.

the sheer amount of education or the substance of the education is the more potent predictor of good quality care. The value of experience, as opposed to education and training, has also been a topic of debate.

With respect to the question of the amount versus the content of education and training, the picture is mixed. Unlike the conclusions of the National Day Care Study that clearly implicated caregivers' child-related education, and not total years of education, as a determinant of preschoolers' social and cognitive development in child care, subsequent research points to both dimensions as contributing to quality child care.

There is ample evidence that specialized training is associated with good quality care. Howes (1983) found that caregivers in centers and family day care homes with more child-related training engaged in more social stimulation and responsiveness than other caregivers. In centers, trained caregivers also showed less negative affect. A national study of family day care homes (Stallings & Porter, 1980) reported similar results for caregiver training. Training was associated with more teaching, helping, dramatic play, and activity that involved interaction with children. Trained family day care providers also showed more comforting behavior and spent less time away from the children than untrained providers. In this study, total years of education showed few relationships with caregiver behavior. Arnett (1987) found associations between specialized caregiver training and more positive interactions with children, lower levels of detachment, and less punitiveness.

Other evidence (Berk, 1985; Clarke-Stewart & Gruber, 1984) suggests that more education is better than less and that the amount and nature of a caregiver's preparation may augment each other such that more highly educated adults who have also received specialized training may be among the most proficient caregivers.

Berk (1985), for example, found that caregivers with at least 2 years of college were more likely than less educated caregivers to display encouragement, teacher direction, and promotion of verbal skills. They were also lower in restrictive behavior. She also found, however, that college-educated caregivers *with a child-related major* showed more indirect guidance, less restriction, and more encouragement of children's self-initiations and verbal expression.

Clarke-Stewart and Gruber (1984) similarly report that the caregiver's formal education and knowledge of child development are associated with higher social and cognitive competence in children attending family day care homes. No significant effects were found for specialized training in child development. Moreover, children in centers with more highly trained

There is ample evidence that specialized training is associated with good quality care.

---

staff were found to be less independent and socially competent than children in centers with less highly trained staff.

The evidence on the contribution of experience is also mixed. Caregivers with more years of experience have been found to engage in less social interaction and cognitive stimulation with infants and toddlers (Ruopp et al., 1979). On the other hand, Howes (1983) found that experienced caregivers were more responsive to children's bids for attention. Stallings and Porter (1980) found no effects for caregiver experience.

Experience is a multifaceted construct. More sensitive measures that are capable of deciphering beneficial features of experience and exploring their relation to competent caregiving are needed, as is substantial refinement of measures of education and training. For example, whereas most studies find a relation between training of caregivers and child outcomes, the content and extent of the training that produces these outcomes are virtually unexplored. This research has also not distinguished the value of education, training, and experience for different levels of child care staff, such as the director of a center, the classroom teachers, and the teacher assistants.

Dynamic measures of classroom quality

While evidence about structural indicators of quality that can be addressed in child care regulations is directly pertinent to licensing authorities and program directors who establish child care policies, these indicators offer few insights into children's actual experiences in child care. Why do more-staff-per-child ratios and small groups promote positive social and cognitive development? What beneficial processes in child care are set in motion in well-structured programs?

The results of the National Day Care Study suggest that structural predictors of quality serve to facilitate constructive interactions between caregivers and children. Several of the studies summarized above imply this as well. What other evidence exists on this issue?

Rubenstein, Howes, and Boyle (1979) followed a sample of 10 children who attended infant care centers. At age 3½, those who had attended centers characterized by high frequencies of social play with caregivers responded more favorably to their mothers following a brief separation than those who were in centers with highly directive caregivers.

Similarly, Carew (1980) followed 23 children who attended child care centers that varied in quality and found that language mastery experiences provided by their caregivers predicted children's performance on IQ and receptive language tests. Golden and his colleagues (1978) also found that 2-year-olds who experienced high levels of cognitive and social stimulation from their child care providers scored higher on measures of social competence and language comprehension when they were 3.

These results are corroborated by those reported by McCartney (1984) in her study of center-based child care in Bermuda. The degree of verbal stimulation provided to the children by their caregivers predicted children's test performance on three measures of language development. In contrast, conversations initiated with peers had a negative influence on language development, leading McCartney to hypothesize that peer talk replaces the more important caregiver talk when fewer adults are on the staff.

In sum, given associations between structural features of child care and caregiver behaviors, the results that link caregivers' social, cognitive, and language interactions with children to child outcomes suggest that the influence of regulatable variables such as ratios and group size is mediated by their effects on caregivers. Structural features of child care appear to affect the dynamic environment that captures children's actual experiences in child care, which in turn predicts children's development in child care.

Contextual features of child care

A relatively recent emphasis in the research on child care quality has expanded the empirical lens to include a variety of child care settings and aspects of quality, such as staff stability, that are not reflected when observations are restricted to single points in time.

The child care setting. Whereas center-based care was studied almost exclusively in the early research on child care, family day care homes are now beginning to be studied, as are in-home care arrangements. This expansion of the child care settings selected as sites for research is highly important. As of 1982, center-based child care constituted 15% of all arrangements used by employed mothers. Family day care, in contrast, constituted 40% of child care arrangements (split about evenly between that provided by a relative and by a nonrelative) and in-home care provided by a nonrelative added another 5.5% (U.S. Bureau of the Census, 1983). It is important to note, however, that center-based care is the most rapidly growing form of care for children of all ages (Hofferth & Phillips, 1987).

Comparing the results of research conducted in different types of care is treacherous given that the measures, the ages and characteristics of the children, and the goals of the research may differ along with the child care setting. Only a few studies have integrated different types of care into a

The loss of an attachment figure can be very painful to a young child.

single research effort (e.g., Benn, 1986; Clarke-Stewart & Gruber, 1984; Howes, 1983; Howes & Rubenstein, 1985). These studies offer the most valid sources of comparison across types of care.

Benn (1986) compared the quality of mother-son attachment for children in family day care homes and in-home arrangements. No differences were found for type of child care setting. Howes (1983) and Howes and Rubenstein (1985) compared children in center and family day care. Both similarities and differences were found. In both types of care smaller groups, higher staff-child ratios, and trained caregivers were associated with better caregiving and child development. Clarke-Stewart and her colleagues (Clarke-Stewart & Gruber, 1984) examined four types of care in Chicago: centers, nursery schools, family day care homes, and in-home care. The results from this study are described fully in Chapter 2, but briefly, Clarke-Stewart concludes that the various types of care present children with qualitatively distinct environments, ranging from home-like to institutional settings with varying degrees of exposure to other children and to educational programs. Very few results were uniform across the four different types of care examined in the Chicago Study.

Staff stability. Developing secure attachment relationships is among the most important developmental tasks for young children. Evidence is clear that children in child care do not replace their attachments to their parents with attachments to their child care providers (Ainslie & Anderson, 1984; Farran, Burchinal, Hutaff, & Ramey, 1984; Kagan, Kearsley, & Zelazo, 1978). At the same time, however, children do get attached to their caregivers (Ainslie & Anderson, 1984; Cummings, 1980; Ricciuti, 1974) and use them as a secure base during the day.

Attachment formation is based in part on the availability and predictability of the caregiver. The loss of an attachment figure can be very painful to a young child. When these observations are juxtaposed with the 40% annual turnover among center-based child care providers and 60% turnover among home-based providers (NAEYC, 1985), there is tremendous cause for concern.

Research on infant and toddler care suggests that very young children differentiate between stable and nonstable caregivers. Rubenstein and Howes (1979) found that twice as much interaction took place in center care between infants and head teachers as between infants and less stable volunteers. Cummings (1980) observed infants during their morning entry into center-based child care. Infants were less resistant to transference from the mother to a stable caregiver and exhibited more positive affect when the mother left, as compared to infants who were transferred to nonstable caregivers.

Howes and Stewart (1987) found that infants and toddlers (age range 11 to 30 months) who had experienced more changes (number of changes ranged from none to five) in child care arrangements were less likely to engage in competent play with peers and objects when observed in their current family day care homes. Moreover, in a study of first-grade children's school adjustment, the stability of prior child care arrangements predicted academic progress (Howes, in press).

Two studies, however, failed to find effects for caregiver stability. Benn (1986) examined caregiver stability in family day care homes and in-home arrangements. No association was found between the number of caregiver changes (ranging from one to eight for boys aged 17 to 21 months) and the quality of the mother-son attachment relationship. Everson, Sarnat, and Ambron (1984) also examined stability in center and family day care home arrangements and found no effects on a broad range of child competence measures.

In sum, when stability is examined within center-based care, there appears to be an association between the consistent presence of an adult caregiver and infants' development in child care. In two studies in which stability was defined as the total number of changes in child care, no association was found. Changes in arrangements and changes in caregivers are quite distinct measures of stability, the first being far more extensive in the degree of change involved. Clearly, this is a very new area of research with much need of further study and clarification.

Joint effects of child care and family environments

Home-rearing (no regular use of other supplemental child care arrangements) has often been used as an implicit standard against which the use of child care has been compared (McCartney & Phillips, in press). Alternatively, child care has frequently been studied as a separate socialization environment apart from children's homes. In reality, childrearing has become a collaborative endeavor with children moving back and forth — many on a daily basis — between their homes and child care. The effects of these two environments may be additive; they may compensate for each other; or some aspects of one may override aspects of the other in positive or negative ways. A full understanding of child development thus requires that both environments be examined.

In addition, there is an important methodological reason to assess the joint effects of child care and family environments. Parents select their

It is likely that parents with different values, finances, and family structures choose child care that varies in form and quality.

children's child care arrangements. It is likely that parents with different values, finances, and family structures choose child care that varies in form and quality.

Howes and Olenick (1986), for example, found that families enrolling their children in low quality child care had more complex and presumably more stressful lives than the families using higher quality care. Moreover, both parents and caregivers of the children in low quality centers were less involved and invested in assuring that their children complied with their requests. This evidence demonstrates that family and child care environments are not independent, making it difficult to attribute child outcomes exclusively to child care or exclusively to family factors. Efforts to tease apart these two realms of influence require, of course, that measures of each be included in research designs. In the absence of this approach the effects of child care on child development may be overestimated (Howes & Olenick, 1986).

Clarke-Stewart and Gruber (1984), for example, report that associations found between children's competence and features of their child care settings, such as group composition and caregiver characteristics, were substantially weakened when variance due to family socioeconomic status (SES) was removed. Kontos's work relating regulatable characteristics of child care centers to quality and children's development similarly revealed that family background variables (SES and family values) significantly predicted developmental outcomes, while structural characteristics of the centers made virtually no contribution to development outcomes (Kontos, 1987; Kontos & Fiene, this volume). Goelman and Pence (1987) have also reported that family variables superseded center quality variables in predicting child language outcomes in a large study of child care in Canada, whereas quality variation in family day care homes was a significant predictor of children's language development. Alternatively, substantial effects of the quality of children's child care centers remained in the Bermuda Study (McCartney, 1984; Phillips, McCartney, & Scarr, 1987) after the influence of the parents' childrearing values was statistically removed.

One possible explanation for this disparate pattern of results concerns the relative range of variation in the family variables versus program quality variables. When the range of families included in the research is more extreme than the range of quality represented by the child care programs, family factors emerge as the more salient influence, whereas the opposite pattern of results appears to emerge when an ample range of child care quality arrangements is included (see subsequent chapters and especially Chapter 7 by Clarke-Stewart for further discussion). This finding has led several investigators to recognize the importance of examining the interrelations between family and quality measures rather than treating them as independent influences on child development.

The Chicago Study provides an example of examining interactive effects. Clarke-Stewart (1984) presents evidence that a combined measure of toys in the home and in child care was more predictive of child development than measures that reflected only the home or child care environments. Howes and Olenick (1986) also found that analyses that incorporated both child care and family influences were more predictive of several child outcomes (e.g., compliance in girls, task resistance in boys) than analyses that took into account only one set of factors.

In a longitudinal study of children in home care, family day care, and center care in Sweden, Cochran (1977), Gunnarsson (1978), and Cochran and Robinson (1983) examined the interaction of structure and process variables in both in-home and out-of-home child care settings. Children's scores on the *Griffiths Scale of Mental Development* were strongly influenced by the interaction of child care structure variables (type of care), child care process and family process variables (social interactions with caregivers and peers), family structure variables (maternal marital status), and child sex. A factor that somewhat restricts the generalizability of these findings is that the subject pool was characterized by unequal proportions of children from one-parent families in the family day care (8%) and center care groups (33%). Nonetheless, this study represents one of the few attempts to examine systematically the interaction of child care and family variables. The investigators concluded that while previous studies

> have tended to view day care as an independent, causal agent operating on the lives of young children . . . the day care experience is better conceptualized as an *intervening* variable [their emphasis] which mediates certain family types on the one hand (two working parents, single parent) and long-term developmental outcomes on the other. (Cochran & Robinson, 1983, p. 61)

Recently, assessments of family influences that relied on broad socioeconomic classifications, childrearing values, and measures of the home environment have been supplemented by more subtle, but perhaps more directly pertinent measures of maternal attitudes toward the use of child care (Everson, Sarnat, & Ambron, 1984; Hock, 1984; Hock, DeMeis, & McBride, 1987). Hock has presented convincing evidence that mothers' attitudes about separation from their children are associated with different patterns of child care use. Employed mothers who have children

It is important to understand parental feelings and attitudes when assessing the effects of different types of care on children.

---

enrolled in child care centers are significantly less concerned about the consequences of maternal separation than are employed mothers who use other forms of care. Hock concludes that it is important to understand parental feelings and attitudes when assessing the effects of different types of care on children (Hock, DeMeis, & McBride, in press).

This approach was taken by Everson and his colleagues (Everson, 1981; Everson, Sarnat, & Ambron, 1984). They examined the mediating influence of mothers' positive or negative disposition to use child care on children's adjustment to child care in both center and family day care arrangements. After the children—all toddlers—had been enrolled in child care for 5 months, the results suggested that the congruence between maternal attitudes and use of child care was a highly significant predictor of children's adjustment. Mothers who relied on child care but were uncomfortable with it and mothers who felt comfortable with the use of child care but were not using it (called *inconsistent mothers*) had children who were more easily upset by a frustrating task, showed greater distress at maternal separation, and were less compliant with their mothers' requests while playing. The inconsistent mothers were also quicker to become angry and impatient with their children.

After 10 months in child care, a different picture emerged. Attitude-behavior consistency was no longer the issue. Attitudes alone predicted child outcomes. Specifically, mothers who were positively disposed toward the use of child care, compared to those who were negatively disposed, had children who were less cooperative with adults, were less compliant with their mothers, and displayed inferior approaches to a problem-solving task, regardless of whether they were in child care or not. Everson concludes, "The specific effects of day care may depend in large measure on maternal attitudes toward day care and other family characteristics" (Everson, Sarnat, & Ambron, 1984, pp. 90–91).

In sum, the combined effects of child care quality and type, the children's child care experience, and their family context need to be considered in future studies of child care. It is entirely possible that family factors (such as parental attitudes about the use of child care) mediate child care choices that, in turn, have differing effects on children. At the very least, inclusion of family-related measures in the study of child care drives home the complexity of identifying where, when, and how quality of care makes a difference in the lives of children.

Conclusions

Research on child care quality has accumulated a vast collection of results during the last 10 years. More than any other aspect of child development research, this literature has driven home the true complexity of child care and the real challenges faced by those who seek to assess its effects on children.

The first challenge for researchers involves selecting a measure of quality — global or discrete, regulatable or more dynamic, a static snapshot measure or one that captures children's and caregivers' movement in and out of child care. The second challenge involves measuring other factors, particularly aspects of the family environment, that affect child development and may interact with, compensate for, or operate completely independently of the influence of child care quality.

In the chapters that follow, five groups of researchers present their efforts to confront these challenges and the results their work has yielded. They have examined different types of child care, in different locations in and out of the United States, and with different populations of children and families. The measures of quality used in these collective studies encompass the full range of options described in this review. Each study placed the developmental consequences of variation in the quality of child care environments in the context of children's home environments. Alison Clarke-Stewart then addresses the central question of how the results of these recent studies confirm, contradict, and extend those of the research reviewed here.

References

Ainslie, R.C., & Anderson, C.W. (1984). Day care children's relationships to their mothers and caregivers: An inquiry into the conditions for the development of attachment. In R.C. Ainslie (Ed.), *Quality variations in daycare* (pp. 98–132). New York: Praeger.

Arnett, J. (1987, April). *Training for caregivers in day care centers*. Paper presented at the biennial meeting of the Society for Research in Child Development, Baltimore, MD.

Benn, R. (1986). Factors promoting secure attachment relationships between employed mothers and their sons. *Child Development, 57,* 1224–1231.

Berk, L. (1985). Relationships of educational attainment, child-oriented attitudes, job satisfaction, and career commitment to caregiver behavior toward children. *Child Care Quarterly, 14,* 103–129.

Bruner, J. (1980). *Under five in Britain*. Ypsilanti, MI: High/Scope.

Childrearing has become a collaborative endeavor with children moving back and forth between their homes and child care.

Carew, J. (1980). Experience and the development of intelligence in young children. *Monographs of the Society for Research in Child Development, 45* (6–7, Serial No. 187).
Clarke-Stewart, A. (1984). Day care: A new context for research and development. In M. Perlmutter (Ed.), *The Minnesota Symposium on Child Psychology, Vol. 17* (pp. 61–100). Hillsdale, NJ: Erlbaum.
Clarke-Stewart, A., & Fein, G.G. (1983). Early childhood programs. In M. Haith & J. Campos (Eds.), *Handbook of child psychology: Vol. 2. Infancy and developmental psychobiology* (pp. 917–1000). New York: Wiley.
Clarke-Stewart, K.A., & Gruber, C. (1984). Daycare forms and features. In R.C. Ainslie (Ed.), *Quality variations in daycare* (pp. 35–62). New York: Praeger.
Cochran, M.M. (1977). A comparison of group day and family childrearing patterns. *Child Development, 48*, 702–707.
Cochran, M.M., & Robinson, J. (1983). Day care, family circumstances and sex differences in children. In S. Kilmer (Ed.), *Advances in early education and day care* (Vol. 3, pp. 46–67). Greenwich, CT: JAI Press.
Cummings, E.H. (1980). Caregiver stability and day care. *Developmental Psychology, 16*, 31–37.
Cummings, M., & Beagles-Ross, J. (1983). Towards a model of infant daycare: Studies of factors influencing responding to separation in daycare. In R.C. Ainslie (Ed.), *Quality variations in daycare* (pp. 159–182). New York: Praeger.
Everson, M.D. (1981). *The impact of day care on the attachment behavior of 12 to 24 month olds.* Unpublished doctoral dissertation, Stanford University, Palo Alto, California.
Everson, M.D., Sarnat, L., & Ambron, S.R. (1984). Day care and early socialization: The role of maternal attitude. In R.C. Ainslie (Ed.), *Quality variations in daycare* (pp. 63–97). New York: Praeger.
Farran, D.C., Burchinal, M., Hutaff, S.E., & Ramey, C.T. (1984). Allegiances or attachments: Relationships among infants and their day care teachers. In R.C. Ainslie (Ed.), *Quality variations in daycare* (pp. 133–158). New York: Praeger.
Field, T. (1980). Preschool play: Effects of teacher:child ratio and organization of classroom space. *Child Study Journal, 10*, 191–205.
Francis, P., & Self, P. (1982). Imitative responsiveness of young children in day care and home settings: The importance of the child to caregiver ratio. *Child Study Journal, 12*, 119–126.
Goelman, H., & Pence, A. (1987). Some aspects of the relationships between family structure and child language development in three types of day care. In D. Peters & S. Kontos (Eds.), *Annual advances in applied developmental psychology, Vol 2: Continuity and discontinuity of experience in child care* (pp. 129–146). Norwood, NJ: Ablex.
Golden, M., Rosenbluth, L., Grossi, M., Policare, H., Freeman, H., & Brownlee, M. (1978). *The New York City Infant Day Care Study.* Medical and Health Research Association of New York City, 40 Worth St., New York, NY 10013.
Gunnarsson, L. (1978). *Children, day care and family care in Sweden: A*

follow-up. Gothenburg, Sweden: University of Gothenburg.

Harms, T., & Clifford, R.M. (1980). *Early Childhood Environment Rating Scale*. New York: Teachers College Press, Columbia University.

Hock, E. (1984). The transition to day care: Effects of maternal separation anxiety on infant adjustment. In R.C. Ainslie (Ed.), *The child and the day care setting* (pp. 183–206). New York: Praeger.

Hock, E., DeMeis, D., & McBride, S. (in press). Maternal separation anxiety: Its role in the balance of employment and motherhood in mothers of infants. In A. Gottfried & A. Gottfried (Eds.), *Maternal employment and children's development: Longitudinal research*. New York: Plenum.

Hofferth, S.L., & Phillips, D.A. (1987). Child care in the United States, 1970 to 1995. *Journal of Marriage and the Family, 49*(3), 559–571.

Howes, C. (in press). Relations between early child care and schooling. *Developmental Psychology*.

Howes, C. (1983). Caregiver behavior in center and family day care. *Journal of Applied Developmental Psychology, 4*, 99–107.

Howes, C., & Olenick, M. (1986). Family and child care influences on toddlers' compliance. *Child Development, 57*, 202–216.

Howes, C., & Rubenstein, J. (1985). Determinants of toddlers' experience in daycare: Age of entry and quality of setting. *Child Care Quarterly, 14*, 140–151.

Howes, C., & Stewart, P. (1987). Child's play with adults, toys and peers: An examination of family and child care influences. *Developmental Psychology, 23*, 423–430.

Kagan, J., Kearsley, R.B., & Zelazo, P.R. (1978). *Infancy: Its place in human development*. Cambridge, MA: Harvard University Press.

Kontos, S. (1987, April). *Day care quality, family background and children's development*. Paper presented at the biennial meeting of the Society for Research in Child Development, Baltimore, MD.

McCartney, K. (1984). The effect of quality of day care environment upon children's language development. *Developmental Psychology, 20*, 244–260.

McCartney, K., & Phillips, D. (in press). *Motherhood and child care*. In B. Birns & D. Hay (Eds.), *Different faces of motherhood*. New York: Plenum.

McCartney, K., Scarr, S., Phillips, D., & Grajek, S. (1985). Day care as intervention: Comparisons of varying quality programs. *Journal of Applied Developmental Psychology, 6*, 247–260.

National Association for the Education of Young Children. (1985). *In whose hands? A demographic factsheet on child care providers*. Washington, DC: NAEYC.

Phillips, D., Scarr, S., & McCartney, K. (1987). Child care quality and children's social development. *Developmental Psychology, 23*, 537–543.

Ricciuti, H. (1974). Fear and the development of social attachments in the first year of life. In M. Lewis & L. Rosenblum (Eds.), *The origins of human behavior: Fear* (pp. 73–106). New York: Wiley.

Ruopp, R., Travers, J., Glantz, F., & Coelen, C. (1979). *Children at the center: Final results of the National Day Care Study.* Cambridge, MA: Abt Associates.

Rubenstein, J.L., & Howes, C. (1979). Caregiving and infant behavior in day care and in homes. *Developmental Psychology, 15,* 1–24.

Rubenstein, J., Howes, C., & Boyle, P. (1979). A two year follow-up of infants in community based day care. *Journal of Child Psychology and Psychiatry, 22,* 209–218.

Rutter, M. (1981). Social-emotional consequences of day care for preschool children. *American Journal of Orthopsychiatry, 51,* 4–28.

Smith, P., & Connolly, K. (1981). *The behavioral ecology of the preschool.* Cambridge, England: Cambridge University Press.

Stallings, J., & Porter, A. (1980). *National Daycare Home Study.* Palo Alto, CA: Stanford Research Institute.

Stith, S.M., & Davis, A.J. (1984). Employed mothers and family day care: A comparative analysis of infant care. *Child Development, 55,* 1340–1348.

U.S. Bureau of the Census. (1983, November). *Child care arrangements of working mothers: June 1982.* Special Studies, Series P-23, No. 129. Washington, DC: U.S. Department of Commerce.

Vandell, D.L., & Powers, C.P. (1983). Day care quality and children's free play activities. *American Journal of Orthopsychiatry, 53,* 493–500.

Zigler, E., & Gordon, E. (1982). *Day care: Scientific and social policy issues.* Boston: Auburn House.

Children whose development was advanced not only had the advantage of being in high quality child care programs but also came from families who gave them support, stimulation, and education.

Chapter 2

Predicting Child Development From Child Care Forms and Features: The Chicago Study

K. Alison Clarke-Stewart

IN THE 1970s, most research on child care contrasted traditional at-home-with-mother care with only one form of alternative care: the child care center. But the question this research was designed to answer—Are children in child care different from those reared exclusively at home?— has today lost its relevance. Now, fully half of the mothers of preschool children in this country use some form of child care for their children. For those parents the important question about child care is not "What is the effect of child care?" but "How can we provide our child with the best possible child care environment?" Their concern, like ours, is with knowing which aspects of child care distinguish the programs in which children do well from those in which they suffer, whether there are differences in the effects of different programs, and just how to recognize a good child care arrangement when they see it.

When any parents choose a child care setting for their offspring they get a package of features. The woman who runs the family day care program down the block is 37 years old, has been taking in children for the last 8 years, and has three toddlers and an infant in her care this week. The university-based nursery school across town has three teachers with Bank Street training, serves 25 children from 2 to 4 years old, boasts a well-equipped playground, and closes for 2 months during the summer. These hypothetical parents must choose between two complex arrangements. They cannot transfer the special warmth they liked in the family day care home to the nursery school, nor bring the more elaborate play equipment and staff of the nursery school to the conveniently located home. Just realizing the complexity of such differences between settings may begin to confuse parents. The parents might, in addition, interview a variety of nannies who would come to the child's home or visit a number of child care centers that would offer them a range of services. These are but a few of the possibilities.

It was to get information that might help parents choose among such child care arrangements, by finding out which aspects of the arrangement were most likely to enhance or to hinder children's development, that my students and I conducted The Chicago Study of Child Care and Development. Parts of this study have been analyzed and published previously (Clarke-Stewart, 1984, 1987; Clarke-Stewart & Gruber, 1984).

The Chicago Study design

We first identified four different child care *forms* that are in popular use: (1) care provided by an individual in the child's own home; (2) care provided in a family day care home; (3) care provided in a part-time nursery school program; and (4) care provided in a full-time child care center program. We then located a sample of 80 families who had a 2- or 3-year-old child in one of these forms of care.

Although we made a concerted effort to recruit approximately equal numbers of children of the same ages (2 and 3 years) for the four child care arrangements, we ended up with more and older children in center arrangements (n = 47, mean age = 39 months) than in home arrangements (n = 34, mean age = 32 months). These differences reflect reality: Center attendance is more likely for older preschool children; parents using centers were more accessible and willing to participate and had child care arrangements that fit our criteria more neatly. Differences in number and children's ages were controlled for statistically in all analyses. For all the children it was their first child care arrangement and they had been in it for 3 to 9 months. All the families were intact and self-supporting.

To ensure variability in the *features* of child care settings — size, adult-child ratio, teacher training, and so on — we took no more than four children from any single setting, so that altogether 63 different settings were represented in the study. Then, to get information about what went on in these different settings, researchers interviewed each child's parents and caregivers at length and made systematic observations totalling 4 to 8 hours for each child. In these observations, the researchers assessed the physical environment — tallying up toys and tricycles, pictures and plants, razor blades and open stairways, dirty dishes and open paint cans — and the social environment — recording who was present and what they did with the child, coding each utterance directed at the child and every occurrence of play, helping, teaching, touching, kissing, and hitting.

In the interviews, the researchers asked parents and caregivers to describe and evaluate the child care arrangements. They also collected background information on the families and the caregivers. This information included the parents' work statuses, occupations, education levels, and incomes, and the caregivers' ages, education levels, training in child development, and knowledge of child development and childrearing (based on their suggested solutions to hypothetical problems in rearing children). As it turned out, most of the mothers of children in in-home care, family day care, and center care were working full-time; most of the mothers of children in nursery school were not employed. Also, the majority of the families in the study were White and of middle-class or professional-class status. This up-scale bias in the sample places a constraint on the generalizability of our findings. Our results represent families of higher-than-average socioeconomic status and, most likely, as a consequence, of better-than-average child care. This is a limited segment of the market, but one that is worth studying, as these are the kinds of families that are most likely to have the resources to make *choices* about child care arrangements. There were no mean differences in socioeconomic status among the four groups in the study.

To assess children's psychological development, we had each child in the study come to the university for a series of tests and observations in a comfortable laboratory playroom. We also observed each child at home several times. From the data we collected in about 10 hours of testing and observing, we compiled a set of eight measures that seemed to reflect important developmental competencies:

1. *Autonomy* (physical independence from mother): How close the child stayed to mother in our testing sessions in the laboratory playroom.

2. *Social reciprocity with mother:* How positive, reciprocal, cooperative, and empathic the child's interactions with mother were in our testing sessions (which included periods of free play and specific tasks meant to measure mother-child interaction).

3. *Social knowledge:* How well the child could take the perspective of another person (e.g., knowing what the other person is thinking or what a picture looks like to another person). How much the child knew about emotional words and situations, and about what is gender-stereotyped behavior for boys and girls.

4. *Sociability with adult stranger:* How friendly, cooperative, sympa-

thetic, helpful, trusting, and likeable the child was with an unfamiliar adult examiner.

5. *Sociability with an unfamiliar peer:* How much positive interaction — talking, playing, cooperating — the child engaged in with an unfamiliar child of the same age and sex and in the same form of child care during the testing session at the university.

6. *Negative behavior to the peer:* How much the child engaged in negative behavior with this unfamiliar child — taking away toys, controlling the child's actions, insulting, refusing to cooperate, withdrawing from or avoiding (hitting did not occur).

7. *Social competence at home:* How obedient, self-confident, sociable, autonomous, assertive, playful, and cheerful the child was at home at dinnertime.

8. *Cognitive ability:* How well the child did on standard tests of language comprehension, verbal fluency, knowledge of concepts, and memory span.

On all these measures except negative to peer, older children scored higher than younger children.

Life in child care

The observations made in the child care settings provided us with a description of the quality of life for children in the four different forms of care. These observations are described here and summarized in Table 2-1.

In-home care

When child care is necessary, the form working parents often claim to prefer is to have an adult come into their home and look after the children there. Department of Labor statistics suggest that this form of care is used by about one-third of the working mothers of preschool children. Often the in-home caregiver is a relative, who may or may not be paid. In our study, one-fourth of these caregivers were unpaid relatives; the rest were not relatives and were paid for their services. The typical caregiver in our study was an older woman (at least 55) with no professional training and limited education: She was unlikely to have graduated from high school or to have taken any courses in child development.

The physical setting — the child's own home — tended to be more adult-oriented than child-oriented. That is, homes had more different types of adult items like drapes, plants, musical instruments, television sets, stereos, and vases (20) than different types of toys and educational

> *Although more emotion was expressed in home-care arrangements, there were fewer planned activities and children spent more time alone or watching TV.*

materials — puzzles, push-pull toys, balls, books, games, and so on (12). They did not usually have specific areas set aside for children's play activities, and there were quite often dirty, messy, and even potentially dangerous features in these homes — overflowing ashtrays, peeling paint, dirty dishes, broken objects, cleaning supplies, medicines, knives (the average was 7 messy or dangerous items).

The in-home caregivers had responsibility for at most two children. This feature offered children frequent opportunities for one-to-one adult-child interaction, and indeed the amount of caregiver-child interaction — physical contact, hugging and kissing, helping, talking, one-to-one teaching — observed in home care was significantly greater than that observed in centers. It also offered children only very limited opportunities to interact with their peers. Any other child present was usually a younger sibling, offering the child only exchanges with a less skilled playmate with whom the child would have been able to play anyway. No child in our study was with another child who was more than a year older than the study child. Visits with other children when with the caregiver — at home, in the park, at a neighbor's — did not greatly augment this contact. Observers found that children with in-home care, on the average, interacted with fewer than two other children.

The activities the child engaged in were also quite limited. Although more emotion was expressed — both positive (smiling, laughing) and negative (crying, hitting) — in home care arrangements, there were fewer planned activities and children spent more time alone or watching TV. In home settings, activities were frequently woven around the normal loose routines of a household — infants needing to be fed and changed, lunch prepared, toys cleaned up, and so on. With only one or two children and few real deadlines to meet, caregivers had little need to create the structural support that routines and organized activities provide. Indeed it is this homey informality and flexibility, combined with a greater sense of their own control over their child's environment, that makes this child care arrangement attractive and reassuring to parents.

Family day care homes

The next form of care, in which the child goes to the family day care provider's house for supervision, is similar to care in the child's own home in many ways. This form of care is used by about one-third of the employed mothers of preschool children in the United States. It is more popular for children younger than 3 than for older children. In our sample, at the beginning of the study, 20 children (at an average age of 32 months) were in

Table 2-1. Characteristics of Child Care Forms

	In-home care	Family day care home	Nursery school	Child care center
Child characteristics				
Number in sample	14	20	22	25
Hours/day in child care	7	7.5	2.5	8
Family socioeconomic status	50	48	48	45
Caregiver characteristics				
Percent who were relatives	25	5	0	0
Average age	47	36	37	30
Years in setting (0–20)[a,b]	1.5	3	3.7	2.6
Education[c]	1	2	3	3
Percent with graduate education	0	5	37	48
Percent with professional experience	8	15	72	62
Percent with some training in child development	14	55	91	96
Percent with more than six courses in child development	7	10	51	52
Physical setting				
Types of toys available (0–25)	12	12	19	19
Types of adult decorations (0–32)	20	18	11	13
Items on messiness checklist (0–12)	5	5	2	2
Items on danger checklist (0–12)	2	2	1	1
Social context				
Children in setting (1–500)[d]	2	6	67	72
Children in class (1–33)	2	5	18	17
Children interacted with (0–29)	1.8	3	10	10
Percent with younger children	40	50	10	15
Percent with older children	0	0	10	15
Percent same as child's ethnicity	11	11	9	9
Heterogeneity of ages, ethnicity, socioeconomic status (combined score)	5.4	9.9	14.2	14.3
Children per caregiver (1–23)[e]	1.7	3.4	5.8	4.0
Adults in setting (1–15)[f]	2.4	2.5	6.3	6.1
Adults in class (1–10)[g]	1.3	1.6	3.3	3.3
Adults interacted with	2.4	1.7	4.5	3.8
Child-child interaction	93	153	119	120
Adult-child interaction	388	179	164	170
Adult-group interaction	5	26	80	75
Total interaction	491	371	375	374

Table 2-1. (Continued)

	In-home care	Family day care home	Nursery school	Child care center
Program/activities				
Structure (checklist)	0.6	1.0	3.5	3.3
Opportunities for learning (ratings)	38	40	73	76
Caregiver to child:				
Talking	329	180	233	235
Physical contact	18	8	13	15
Helping	8	4	6	6
Teaching	22	13	20	20
Lessons	14	26	32	30
Reading	10	4	43	40
Demands	50	36	48	48
Playing	65	28	6	10
Child:				
Play with peers	38	97	100	102
Solitary play	100	65	2	0
TV watching	79	50	0	0
Solitary play with object	146	138	122	122
Positive emotion	82	75	79	79
Negative emotion	23	11	16	16

[a] Numbers in parentheses represent observed ranges.
[b] Only 3 caregivers had been in their settings longer than 10 years.
[c] 1 = high school; 2 = some college; 3 = college graduate
[d] Only 9 centers had more than 100 children.
[e] Only 3 classes had more than 14 children per caregiver.
[f] Only 4 centers had more than 9 adults.
[g] Only 4 classes had more than 6 adults.

family day care homes; one year later, 7 were in the same type of arrangement. On the average, children in family day care homes spent 7½ hours a day there. The women who ran these family day care homes were significantly younger than the in-home caregivers (average age 36 years versus 47). Like the in-home caregivers, they were unlikely to have had professional child care experience. They did have more education — most had taken some college-level courses — and more specialized training — half had taken at least one course in child development — but their level of education was still significantly below that of the teachers in the center programs. Although it is common for family day care to be provided by a relative, this was not so in our study. Only one family day care provider was a relative and only two were unpaid.

Family day care homes were identical to the children's own homes in the variety of toys, the predominance of adult decorations, and the messiness and dangerousness of the physical environment they provided. At first glance this may be surprising. One might expect that a facility in the business of providing child care would be more child centered than children's own homes. But a family day care home is fundamentally a home, even when it is stretched to take in more children. It functions as a home for the family who lives there, and most providers, even caregivers who try to make a profit, strive to incorporate their young charges into their own family's routines rather than making their home an institution.

The main way in which family day care homes differ from children's own homes is in the social milieu they provide. In the typical family day care home in our study there were 5 children (the number ranged from 3 to 10). Thus family day care homes provided significantly more varied opportunities for interaction with different children than own-home care. These children represented a mix of racial, ethnic, and social class backgrounds, but they were all young. None of the family day care homes in which we observed had children more than a year older than the child in the study, so children's peer encounters were, as in own-home care, limited to those with relatively unskilled playmates.

Nursery schools

The third form of care was that provided by nursery schools. Nursery schools have grown steadily in popularity since they began in this country in the 1920s. Today, most middle-class parents consider it desirable to provide their 3- and 4-year-old children with some kind of nursery school experience, and more than one-third of them do so. In our study, 22 children were attending nursery school at the beginning and, despite some attrition in the total sample, 39 were in nursery school one year later.

The typical nursery school teacher was the same age as the typical family day care provider (37 years old), but there the similarity ended. These women were child care professionals. All were college graduates and more than 90% had formal training in child development at college. They had been in their present jobs an average of nearly 4 years, longer than caregivers in any other form of care in the study.

The physical settings in the nursery schools we observed were neat and orderly, free of hazards, with only a couple of messy features per setting. Unlike both home care settings, they had areas set aside for different kinds of play and had more types of toys and educational materials (19) than

Group programs offered children more opportunities for education, interaction, and socialization than home-care programs.

---

types of adult decorations (11).

In the nursery schools, children were exposed to at least three different adults and, instead of a lone sibling or a handful of fellow toddlers to play with, a large group of other children. The average class size was 18 and our children were observed to interact with 10 of these children, on the average, during a 2-hour observation period. Not surprisingly, children in nursery schools participated in one-to-one interaction with an adult less frequently than children in either type of home care, but they participated in group activities with the teacher, listening to the teacher read, talk, or teach, more frequently than the home care children. Nursery school children also had more frequent and varied experiences with other children — playing, chatting, learning — and the children with whom they interacted included some who were older, offering them more mature playmates and models, and who represented a wider range of ethnic and social class backgrounds.

Nursery school programs were more likely to have scheduled activities, clearly defined play areas with associated routines, and a specific curriculum: traditional, open, Piagetian, Montessori, or DISTAR. These programs were evaluated by our observers and by the caregivers themselves as offering children more opportunities for education, interaction, and socialization than home care programs.

Child care centers

The fourth form of care, in full-time child care centers, was basically the same as care in nursery schools, but extended to full time by meals, naps, and periods of free play. The only differences we observed between these two forms of care — apart from the longer hours — were that the teachers in child care centers tended to be younger (30 years old on the average), more educated, and had been working in their present jobs a shorter time (2½ years).

In brief, the four forms of child care differed in reasonable and expected ways on all the dimensions we measured. In terms of caregiver characteristics, in-home caregivers were the oldest, were the least well-educated and professionally experienced or trained, had been in the setting the shortest time, and were most likely to be related to the child. Family day care home providers were younger and more highly educated than in-home caregivers; about half had some specialized training in child development. Nursery school teachers were the same age as the family day care home providers but more highly educated; about half had extensive training in child development; they had been in their present positions for the longest time and were most likely to have professional experience. Child care center staff were the youngest and the most highly trained and educated. There was no difference between groups in how well the caregivers did on our assessment of their knowledge of child development and childrearing.

In terms of the physical setting, the differences observed were between homes and centers. Homes (child's or family day care provider's) had fewer types of toys and educational materials available and more adult decorations and safety hazards. Centers (nursery schools or child care centers) had more types of toys and educational materials and fewer adult items and hazards.

In terms of the social context, in-home care, family day care, and center care all differed from each other. In in-home care, the child had only one or two other children to play with; in family day care, five or six other children; in center care, a class of 18. Children had more different adults to interact with in nursery school (three) and center programs (six) than children in home programs (one or two). The adult-child ratios, on the average, were 1:6 in nursery school classes, 1:4 in child care centers, 1:3½ in day care homes, and 1:1½ with in-home caregivers. Perhaps as a consequence of these differences in numbers, children participated in one-to-one interaction with the caregiver most often in in-home care and least often in a nursery school. In nursery schools children were more likely to listen to the caregiver as part of a group than in the other settings. Children spent the most time interacting with other children in family day care homes.

In terms of the program and activities in the different child care forms, the big difference, again, was between homes and centers. Centers were more likely than homes to have a structured schedule and curriculum and to provide opportunities for learning, including stories and songs. In home settings, especially with a caregiver in their own home, children spent more time alone or watching TV, expressed more emotion, played more, and had more physical contact with the caregiver. Family day care homes were like centers in the frequency of peer play.

Child care forms and child development

To find out how child care affects children's development, we first analyzed the differences on the child development measures for children in these different forms of care. Details of these and other analyses described in this chapter can be found elsewhere (Clarke-Stewart, 1984, 1987; Clarke-Stewart & Gruber, 1984). In all these analyses children's ages were statistically controlled so that age differences do not confound the results. The differences on the child development measures were strong and statistically significant.

Children attending nursery school programs consistently scored higher, especially on assessments of cognitive ability, social knowledge, and sociability with the adult stranger. These children were 6 to 9 months more advanced than children in home care (see Figures 2-1, 2-2, and 2-3). Least advanced were children with caregivers in their own homes. These children never scored highest on any of our tests and they were significantly more likely than children in centers to behave negatively toward the peer. Children in family day care homes had the distinction of scoring

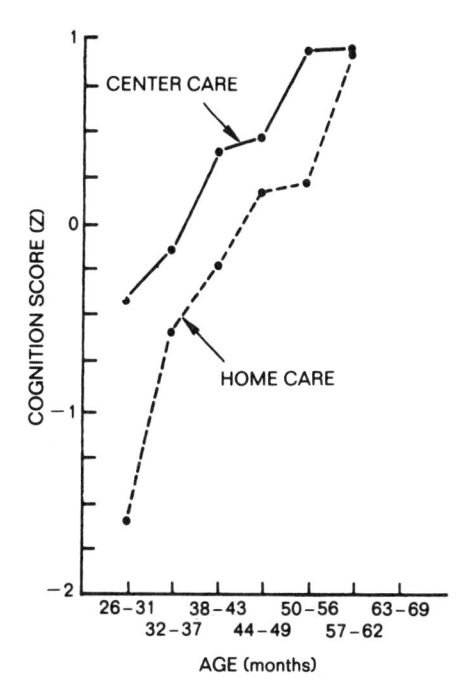

Figure 2-1. Mean scores on cognitive development measures for children in home care (with in-home caregivers or in family day care homes) and in center care (in centers or nursery schools); sample divided cross-sectionally into 6-month age periods

Children with untrained caregivers in their own home, with one other child (usually younger) at most, and with no educational program did not excel in any domain of competence.

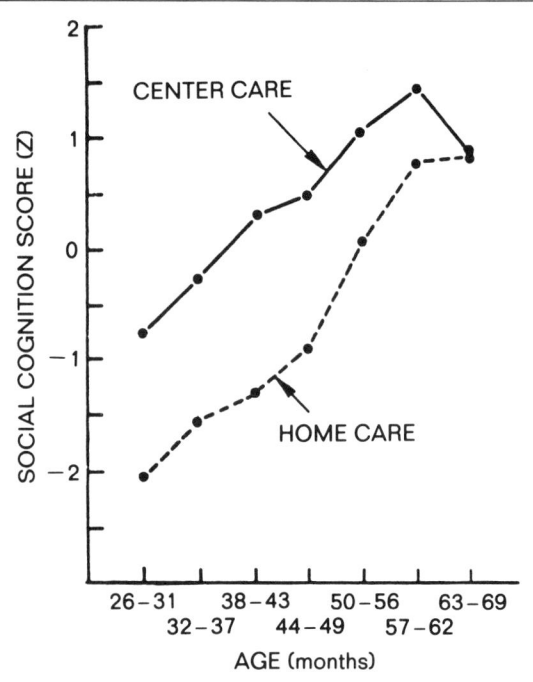

Figure 2-2. Mean scores on social cognition measures for children in home care (with in-home caregivers or in family day care homes) and in center care (in centers or nursery schools); sample divided cross-sectionally into 6-month age periods

highest on sociability with the unfamiliar peer, but they were lowest on the measure of independence from mother. Children from full-time child care centers were the most independent of their mothers in terms of physical distance and the highest in terms of social reciprocity.

Thus we see that the four forms of child care were associated with predictable patterns of competence in the children attending them. The educational orientation of the nursery school was reflected in advanced cognition and adult-oriented competence. The lengthier separation of mothers and children using full-time child care centers was reflected in the child's greater physical independence from mother coupled with more involved social interactions with her. Children from family day care homes, who had less familiarity than center children with an institutional setting, stayed closer to their mothers in our university setting, but, consistent with their opportunity for intimate social interaction with

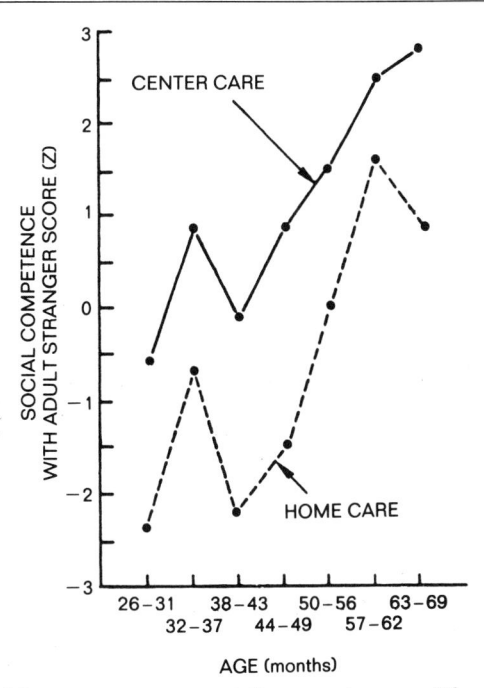

Figure 2-3. Mean scores on social competence with adult strangers for children in home care (with in-home caregivers or in family day care homes) and in center care (in centers or nursery schools); sample divided cross-sectionally into 6-month age periods

peers, played more comfortably, cooperatively, and actively with an unfamiliar child than children with in-home caregivers. Children with untrained caregivers in their own home, with one other (usually younger) child at most, and with no educational program did not excel in any domain of competence.

Child development and child care features

These findings apply to groups of children in different forms of child care. But of course there were also variations *within* these forms. All centers are not created equal, and neither are home settings. To find out how variation within child-care forms is related to children's development, we analyzed associations between the child development measures and

For the preschool child, there may be benefits from having more people around than just a solitary caregiving adult.

features of the particular settings children were attending. This was done separately for children in home care (with in-home caregivers or in family day care homes) and in center programs (in nursery schools or child care centers).

Features of home child care

In the home settings, significant differences in children's development were found to be related to who was present, what they did with the child, and how the physical environment was arranged.

Caregiver characteristics and activities. There was no relation between children's competence and the amount of formal training in child development the caregiver had—perhaps because so few of the home caregivers had extensive training. But children generally did better when the provider was more highly educated and knew more about child development. Children from family day care homes did better in our assessments of intellectual and social competence when the caregiver had more one-to-one conversations with them, and when she touched, read to, and gave more directions to them. Children with in-home caregivers and no other children present did better when the caregivers interacted with them *less*. Because the overall amount of caregiver-child interaction when there were no other children present was higher than when there was more than one child, one might speculate that the level of caregiver interaction in these single-child settings got to the point of being *too* much.

Children in both in-home care and family day care homes were more competent when the *quality* of their interactions with the caregiver was more responsive. Children whose interactions with the caregiver were more positive and responsive, though not more frequent, were also observed to have more positive, reciprocal, and cooperative interactions with their mothers in our laboratory assessment. Children who received less teaching, directing, and controlling from their caregivers stayed physically closer to their mothers in our laboratory observation—an immature behavior. Children with older caregivers (at least 50) were more successful on tests of social knowledge, but children with younger caregivers were more sociable in their interactions with adult strangers who came to visit them.

Social context/group composition. The number and kinds of other children who were present in the home care settings also were related to how competent children were. Children generally did better on our assessments of social knowledge and social competence when the number of other children present was small (one to five) and the amount the child

> *Children were developmentally advanced when the home was neat and orderly, was organized around their activities, and contained fewer adult-oriented decorative items.*

interacted with them was moderate. Children who spent a lot of time interacting with, imitating, or simply watching other children (especially groups of children and younger children and infants) did less well on our tests of competence, particularly social competence with the unfamiliar peer. The ethnic and social class heterogeneity of the group and the adult-child ratio were not significantly related to children's competence.

Physical setting. Finally, the organization of the physical environment in the home was related to our measures of children's competence. Children were developmentally advanced when the home was neat and orderly, was organized around their activities, and contained fewer adult-oriented decorative items (with perhaps less need for restrictions — "Stay away from that plant!" "Don't touch that vase!"). Just providing more different toys was not in itself helpful, however, and, in fact, when children spent more time playing alone with toys and objects than interacting with the caregiver they did less well in our assessments of competence and social reciprocity. The more time children spent alone in the room, also, the worse they did. How much time children spent watching television during our observations was not related to their competence.

Other studies. These relations are generally supported by the handful of other studies of children in family day care homes. Such studies show that the quality of care and children's development are better in those homes where the provider has a professional self-concept, is knowledgeable about child development, and is able to interact well with the children; where the number of children is small; and where the physical environment is suitable for children's activities (Espinosa, 1980; Fosburg et al., 1980; Howes, 1983; Howes & Rubenstein, 1981; Kagan, Fargo, Rauch, & Crowell, 1977). The research on home-reared children's development (reviewed by Clarke-Stewart, 1977, 1979; Wachs & Gruen, 1982) similarly reveals relations between development and the following factors: the caregiver's (parent's) level of education, knowledge about children, and interaction (verbal, responsive, informative, nonauthoritarian) with the child; a smaller number of children in the setting (the family); and a physical environment (home) that is not crowded, restrictive, or chaotic.

Features of center care

Social context/group composition. The associations observed in home settings suggest that for the preschool child there may be benefits from having more people around than just a solitary caregiving adult. Child care centers and nursery schools never have just a solitary caregiver. In centers, it is generally believed, the danger is having too many people,

The more the teacher directed, demanded, controlled, and punished children, the worse they performed on our tests of cognition and cooperation with adult strangers.

not too few. Our study supports this belief: Children in large *centers*, with large numbers of adults and children, did less well on the tests of social competence. There were some advantages of size however. Children in larger *classes*, although also less sociable with peer and adult strangers, did better on tests of social knowledge and were less likely to behave negatively toward the unfamiliar peer in our laboratory assessment — perhaps because they had learned that such behavior is not allowed in more crowded classrooms.

A parallel advantage was related to having a large number of children per teacher: Children in classes with more children per teacher were more cooperative with peers and adults in our assessments than children in classes with a higher adult-child ratio. Bigger is thus neither uniformly better nor inevitably worse.

Being in a more diverse and heterogeneous group of children was associated, on the down side, with having a lower level of social knowledge, less independence from mother, less social competence with a peer and with an adult visitor and, on the up side, with exhibiting less negative behavior with the peer. As in home care, children in center programs who spent a great deal of their time playing with their classmates were less sociable with the unfamiliar peer in our assessments. Unlike the home care children, center children who played more with their peers were more positive with their mothers. If their classmates were responsive and older and set a mature model that children could watch, or played with the child at a more sophisticated level (e.g., dramatic play rather than simple associative play), then children were advanced in cognitive and social competence. Not surprisingly, children whose interchanges with their classmates were more aggressive and negative were less competent in our tests at the university.

Caregiver characteristics and activities. As far as the qualifications and training of the caregivers in centers went, results were mixed. When the teacher was older, had been in the center longer, and was more highly trained in and more knowledgeable about child development, children scored higher on tests of cognitive abilities. But they were less independent of their mothers and less sociable with peers, parents, and adult strangers. Being more socially competent was related to having a teacher with a higher level of overall education but less academic training specifically in child development.

This is a provocative finding, suggesting that a narrowly focused, academically trained teacher may facilitate children's academic intellectual abilities at the expense of their social skills. The more the teacher

Children who were more competent in these tests attended programs where they were given freedom to learn.

---

directed, demanded, controlled, and punished children, the worse they performed on our tests of cognition and cooperation with adult strangers. Children who were more competent in these tests attended programs where they were given freedom to learn. The teacher read to the children, offered them choices, and encouraged them to manipulate materials on their own. She did not interact with children by hugging, holding, or helping.

The number of explanatory or informative sentences spoken by the teacher to children and the time the teacher actually spent giving children lessons were, surprisingly, not related to children's cognitive development. Children who heard more explanatory or informative sentences and who received more directions from the teacher were, however, more competent with the unfamiliar peer. This suggests that the instruction and direction the children got in their child care classes were more likely to be about how to get along with peers than about what comes before 7 or after C. Children who had more interaction with the teacher (touching, talking, teaching, or reading) were less positive and cooperative with their mothers.

Physical setting and curriculum. When the physical environment was safer and more orderly, and contained more varied and stimulating toys, decorations, and educational materials appropriately organized into activity areas, children did better on tests of cognitive skills and social competence with adult strangers.

Other studies. Previous research has revealed positive associations between preschool children's cognitive competence and the following child care features: caregivers' training in child development, moderately structured (i.e., teacher-directed, intellectually demanding) experiences in the program, and the presence of a relatively small group of children (Connolly & Smith, 1978; Johnson, Ershler, & Bell, 1980; McCartney, 1984; Miller & Dyer, 1975; Rubenstein & Howes, 1983; Ruopp, Travers, Glantz, & Coelen, 1979; Sylva, Roy, & Painter, 1980; Tizard, Philps, & Plewis, 1976; Tizard, Pinkerton, & Carmichael, 1982).

Advantages for peer interaction have been linked to teacher direction, fantasy play, small groups, older children, and well-organized play spaces (Beller, Litwok, & Sullivan, undated; Field, 1980; Howes, 1983; Huston-Stein, Friedrich-Cofer, & Susman, 1977; Smith, Dalgliesh, & Herzmark, 1981; Sylva et al., 1980). These findings are consistent with ours. So is the finding from the National Day Care Study (Ruopp et al., 1979) that a high adult-child ratio, that supposed sine qua non of high quality child care, is not necessarily a predictor of better outcomes for preschool children.

When the physical environment was safer and more orderly, and contained more varied and stimulating toys, decorations, and educational materials

Summing up

Results at the level of associations between the features of particular child care settings and the development of individual children are more complex and difficult to summarize than the broad patterns related to child care forms. There are no simple statements about good and bad features, it seems. What is good or bad depends on the setting and the people: Different associations between features and development were found in home and center settings, with a single child or a group. What is good or bad depends on the way the feature is defined: *size*, for example, was good or bad depending on whether it was defined as center size, class size, or adult-child ratio. What is good or bad depends on the measure of child development used: Different patterns were found for social competence with peers and adults, in tests of knowledge and observations of behavior. Finally, what is good or bad is not always related to a child development measure in a simple, linear way in which more is better and less is worse. A moderate level of the feature often turned out to be optimal. At present, the results of research on child care features may have raised more issues than they have resolved. What then can we conclude about the relations between features of programs and children's development? The following were the clearest links we observed.

Caregiver characteristics

Education. A higher level of caregiver education was related to a higher level of children's social competence.

Training. A higher level of specialized college training in child development was related to a higher level of cognitive competence — but to a lower level of social competence.

Quality of interaction with child. A higher level of responsive, informative, and accepting caregiver behavior was related to children's overall competence.

Amount of interaction. There was no simple association between the amount of interaction with the caregiver and children's competence.

Content of interaction. More frequent reading and giving choices to the child were related to the child's higher competence; more frequent helping, holding, hugging, controlling, and punishing were related to the child's lower competence.

appropriately organized into activity areas, children did better on tests of cognitive skills and social competence with adult strangers.

Group composition

Number of children. A moderate number of children in the group was related to higher social competence.

Adult-child ratio. More adults per child was related to lower social competence.

Amount of interaction with children. A high frequency of play with other children in the child care setting was related to lower social competence with the unfamiliar peer in the assessment situation.

Age of children. The opportunity to watch and interact with older children was related to higher competence; the presence of younger children and infants was related to lower competence.

Physical setting

Order and structure. Neatness, orderliness, safety, and structure in the physical environment was related to higher levels of competence.

Stimulation. The opportunity to interact with varied toys and educational materials was related to higher levels of cognitive competence.

Interpreting child care/child development links

Although there were some consistent and sensible links between children's experiences in their child care settings and how they performed in standard situations that reflected their abilities outside the child care setting, there is one critical constraint on interpreting what these links mean. One cannot conclude that simply putting children in a well-equipped center with a well-educated teacher and a small class of mature, responsive children will automatically promote their development. The associations we observed between forms and features of child care and children's development are just that—associations. We cannot be sure that is was the program's forms and features that *caused* the differences in children's development. The children were not randomly assigned to the programs where we observed them. Their parents had deliberately *selected* these programs for them. Perhaps parents put their children in better programs *because* the children were already more advanced developmentally. Parents who put their children in nursery schools and child care centers were likely to say that they chose these programs because

More was not always better, and less was not always worse. A moderate level of the feature often turned out to be optimal.

they offered the children educational opportunities. What this suggests is that in this study children whose development was more advanced not only had the advantage of being in high quality child care programs but also came from families who gave them support, stimulation, and education at home. There was evidence in the study that child care programs had *some* direct effects on development. High quality child care predicted not just children's levels of cognitive development but also the *gains* in cognitive development the children made after they were placed in the programs. But clearly the child care programs were not operating alone. Child care is simply part of the child's total milieu. Children do not live by child care alone—no matter how fitting its form or how fine its features.

References

Beller, E.K., Litwok, E., & Sullivan, K. (Undated). *An observational study of interaction in day care.* Unpublished manuscript, Temple University, Philadelphia.

Clarke-Stewart, A. (1977). *Child care in the family: A review of research and some propositions for policy.* New York: Academic.

Clarke-Stewart, K.A. (1979). Evaluating parental effects on child development. In L. Shulman (Ed.), *Review of research in education* (Vol. 6, pp. 47–119). Itasca, IL: Peacock.

Clarke-Stewart, A. (1984). Day care: A new context for research and development. In M. Perlmutter (Ed.), *The Minnesota Symposium on Child Psychology* (Vol. 17, pp. 61–100). Hillsdale, NJ: Erlbaum.

Clarke-Stewart, A. (1987). The social ecology of early childhood. In N.E. Eisenberg (Ed.), *Contemporary topics in developmental psychology* (pp. 292–318). New York: Wiley.

Clarke-Stewart, K.A., & Gruber, C. (1984). Day care forms and features. In R.C. Ainslie (Ed.), *The child and the day care setting* (pp. 35–62). New York: Praeger.

Connolly, K.J., & Smith, P.K. (1978). Experimental studies of the preschool environment. *International Journal of Early Childhood, 10,* 86–95.

Espinosa, L. (1980). *An ecological study of family day care.* Unpublished doctoral dissertation, University of Chicago.

Field, T.M. (1980). Preschool play: Effects of teacher/child ratios and organization of classroom space. *Child Study Journal, 10,* 191–205.

Fosburg, S., Hawkins, P.D., Singer, J.D., Goodson, B.D., Smith, J.M., & Brush, L.R. (1980). *National Day Care Home Study* (Contract No. HEW 105-77-1051). Cambridge, MA: Abt Associates.

Howes, C. (1983). Caregiver behavior in center and family day care. *Journal of Applied Developmental Psychology, 4,* 99–107.

Howes, C., & Rubenstein, J.L. (1981). Toddler peer behavior in two types of day care. *Infant Behavior and Development, 4,* 387–394.

Huston-Stein, A., Friedrich-Cofer, L.K., & Susman, E.J. (1977). The relation of classroom structure to social behavior, imaginative play, and self-regulation of

economically disadvantaged children. *Child Development, 48,* 908–916.
Johnson, J.E., Ershler, J., & Bell, C. (1980). Play behavior in a discovery-based and a formal-education preschool program. *Child Development, 51,* 271–274.
Kagan, M., Fargo, J., Rauch, M.D., & Crowell, D. (1977). *Infant satellite nurseries: Family day care with a difference.* National Institutes of Mental Health Grant Report No. MH 21129.
Miller, L.B., & Dyer, J.L. (1975). Four preschool programs: Their dimensions and effects. *Monographs of the Society for Research in Child Development, 40* (5–6, Serial No. 162).
McCartney, K. (1984). Effect of quality of day care environment on children's language development. *Developmental Psychology, 20,* 244–260.
Rubenstein, J.L., & Howes, C. (1983). Social-emotional development of toddlers in day care: The role of peers and of individual differences. *Advances in Early Education in Day Care, 3,* 13–45.
Ruopp, R., Travers, J., Glantz, F., & Coelen, C. (1979). *Children at the center: Final results of the National Day Care Study.* Cambridge, MA: Abt Associates.
Smith, P.K., Dalgleish, M., & Herzmark, G. (1981). A comparison of the effects of fantasy play tutoring and skills tutoring in nursery classes. *International Journal of Behavioral Development, 4,* 421–441.
Sylva, K., Roy, C., & Painter, M. (1980). *Child watching at play group and nursery school.* London: Grant McIntyre.
Tizard, B., Philps, J., & Plewis, I. (1976). Play in pre-school centres—II. Effects on play of the child's social class and of the educational orientation of the centre. *Journal of Child Psychology and Psychiatry, 17,* 265–274.
Tizard, B., Pinkerton, G., & Carmichael, H. (1982). Adults' cognitive demands at home and at a nursery school. *Journal of Child Psychology and Psychiatry, 23,* 105–116.
Wachs, T.D., & Gruen, C.E. (1982). *Early experience and human development.* New York: Plenum.

Higher quality programs were also associated with greater verbal interaction between caregivers and children, as well as lower rates of caregiver turnover.

Chapter 3

Dimensions and Effects of Child Care Quality: The Bermuda Study

Deborah A. Phillips, Sandra Scarr, and Kathleen McCartney

CHILD CARE has become routine for parents rearing children now. With this social change has come recognition of the fact that child care environments vary greatly. Studies that treat child care as a homogeneous phenomenon are thus outdated and misleading. Today's questions focus on identifying the developmental consequences of attending child care that varies widely in quality. An additional, relatively new focus of child care literature is on the joint effects of child care and family variables.

The study presented here examines the relation between child care quality in center-based care and children's development. The contribution of children's child care experience and family background was also examined for the two developmental outcomes: social and language competencies. The outcome measures emphasize social and language development because of their significance for preschool children. We deliberately excluded cognitive outcomes given the wide consensus that child care has neutral or positive effects on cognitive development (Belsky, Steinberg, & Walker, 1982; Clarke-Stewart & Fein, 1983). On the other hand, there is a continuing controversy about the effects of child care on children's social skills and a dearth of information about effects on their verbal skills.

The design of the study was guided by theoretical, methodological, and policy concerns. With respect to theory, studies of child care can inform basic questions about environmental influences on child development. Because child care providers are unrelated to the children in their care, research on the effects of child care quality can provide a relatively clear-cut assessment of the environmental malleability of development when appropriate controls for parental selection of child care are included.

We also sought to rectify several of the methodological shortcomings

Children's performance on the measures of intellectual and language development were influenced primarily by staff-child ratios and amounts of caregiver-child verbal interaction.

that have plagued the child care literature. Samplings of children and of child care programs are vitally important to the generalizability of the research results. Whereas many prior researchers have studied children from middle-class families in relatively high quality, university-based arrangements, we studied representative center care that varied widely in quality and enrolled children with large differences in family background and child care experience.

A second methodological problem concerns parental selection of child care. Howes and Olenick (1986) have demonstrated that families served by low- and high-quality care differ significantly on measures of family stress. Because parents select children's child care environments, any effects found for differences in quality could result from differences in the families that place their children in low- and high-quality programs. Children's experiences in child care—their age of entry and length of time in care—may also vary systematically with the quality of their child care environments, making it difficult to distinguish effects that are attributable to quality rather than to experience. This study was designed to control for these two alternative sources of influence—child care experience and family background—prior to examining the effects of child care quality.

Measurement of quality in child care was a relatively new endeavor at the time this research was designed. We chose to include several assessments of quality to address distinct issues. A global assessment of quality provided the broadest test of whether differences in child care environments affect child development. We also discovered that subscales from the global measure, such as the quality of personal care and opportunities for creative activities, were highly interrelated, making efforts to tease apart their influence somewhat suspect.

Given our interest in informing policy issues associated with child care quality, we examined structural aspects amenable to state regulation. Staff-child ratios, the director's years of experience in child care, and caregiver turnover rates were selected for study on the basis of their policy relevance and their variability in the study centers. Caregiver training, a significant predictor of child outcomes in prior research (Ruopp, Travers, Glantz, & Coelen, 1979), showed minimal variation in these centers, and was thus not included.

These policy measures, however, tell us very little about the processes that account for associations between quality and child development. Verbal interactions between adults and children were thus included as a third type of quality assessment designed to capture the dynamic environment of child care.

In sum, the principal aims of the study were

1. to examine the consequences for development of the *quality* of the center a child attends,

2. to identify specific indicators of quality — staff-child ratios, director experience, caregiver turnover, and verbal interactions among caregivers and children — that may account for results obtained when quality is treated as a global construct, and

3. to determine whether associations between quality and child outcomes are affected by the children's child care experience or family background.

Method

Child care settings

Bermuda was the site for this research — a feature that has several serendipitous benefits. First, approximately 85% of Bermudian children spend the majority of their day in some form of supplemental care by the time they are 2 years of age. This reduces potential biases associated in other cultures with the mere use of child care. Second, each of the nine child care centers in Bermuda that had been in operation for more than 4 years and that accepted children from infancy through the preschool years agreed to participate in the study, thus assuring wide variation in program quality and in the children's family environments and experiences in child care. Eight of the centers were privately owned; one was government run and served predominantly low-income families.

Subjects

We asked the parents of all children 3 years and older who had attended one of the nine centers for 6 months or more (not necessarily full time) if they and their children would participate in the study. A total of 166 families agreed, with only 15 refusals. The children ranged in age from 36 to 68 months; 130 were Black and 36 were White. Fathers were present in 68% of the households; maternal education ranged from 5 to 22 years; and the mothers' occupations ranged from 6 to 62 on the National Opinion Research Corporation Prestige Scale. The average age of entry into child care was 19 months for the participating children.

Measures

Child care quality. The quality of the child care environment was assessed in three ways. First, we used Harms and Clifford's (1980) Early Childhood Environment Rating Scale (ECERS) to obtain observational ratings of quality on the six dimensions that pertain directly to the *child* environment: personal care, creative activities, language/reasoning, fine/gross motor, social development, and furnishings/display. High intercorrelations among the subscales (rs ranged from .60 to .92) led us to rely exclusively on the total scale score.

Second, we obtained structural indicators of quality from an extensive interview with each program director, based on the Day Care Environment Inventory (Prescott, Kritchevsky, & Jones, 1972). The interview focused on descriptive aspects of the child care facility, staff, and program. From this interview, the director's years of experience, the child-staff ratio, and the caregiver turnover rate were selected for analysis.

Third, we assessed verbal interactions between adults and children using an observational coding system (see McCartney, 1984) in which eight children per center were observed for six 10-minute segments each. The number of functional utterances directed to children by caregivers provided the verbal environment measure.

Child development. Social development was assessed using parent and caregiver ratings on two standardized measures: the preschool form of the Classroom Behavior Inventory (Schaefer & Edgerton, 1978), which assesses social competence through factors for intelligence, considerateness, sociability, task orientation, and dependence; and the Preschool Behavior Questionnaire (Behar & Stringfield, 1974), which assesses social adjustment through ratings for aggression, anxiety, and hyperactivity. Verbal intelligence was assessed with the revised Peabody Picture Vocabulary Test (PPVT-r) (Dunn, 1979). Language development was assessed using three different strategies: standardized test results from the Preschool Language Assessment Instrument (PLAI) (Blank, Rose, & Berlin, 1978), caregiver ratings from the Adaptive Language Inventory (ALI) (Feagans & Farran, 1979), and research team ratings of free-speech samples collected during an experimental communication task.

Family environment. Family environment measures were derived from parent interviews that included demographic questions (e.g., family income, age and education of parents), as well as items from the Parent as Educator Interview (Schaefer & Edgerton, 1977) designed to assess paren-

> *Parents who placed a high value on social skills and a low value on conformity selected higher quality child care centers.*

tal values about child learning and development. We selected our final measures of the family environment based on their association with the ECERS measures of overall quality to control for center selection biases. The two family variables that were significant predictors of program quality were *values social skills*, a positive predictor of ECERS, and *values conformity*, a negative predictor. In other words, parents who placed a high value on social skills and low value on conformity selected higher quality child care centers than did other parents.

Child care experience. The parent interview elicited the child's age of first entry into child care and the total length of time the child had been enrolled in child care.

Procedure

Between March and June 1980, two researchers visited each of the nine child care centers on at least three different days to administer the director's interview, collect the verbal environment data, and rate program quality on the ECERS. During the initial visit researchers distributed the social measures and the ALI to the caregivers. The two additional program visits by two researchers were required to collect observational data on the verbal interactions between children and caregivers. Eighteen Bermudian college students, naive to the purpose of the study, conducted the family interviews to obtain the parent ratings on the measures of social development and the information about family environment and child care history. Four of these students administered the PPVT-r, the PLAI, and the communication task to the children in their child care centers.

Data analysis strategy

The general strategy for the quality analyses involved controlling for the influence of the child's age, family environment, and child care experience before estimating the contribution of child care quality to children's development. The hierarchical regression model used to implement this strategy is presented in Table 3-1. This is a conservative assessment of the influence of quality, given that all variation in the developmental outcomes attributable to the family environment and child care experience variables entered in the first three equations is removed before the variation associated with quality is assessed. The model was computed separately for each of the parent and caregiver ratings of social development and for the four measures of verbal intelligence and language development.

Table 3-1. **Hierarchical Regression of Developmental Outcomes on Age, Family Background, Child Care Experience, and Overall Quality**

	Change in R^2		
Measure	Family environment: Values conformity/ values social skill	Experience: Age at entry/ time in care	Quality: ECERS
Considerateness			
Parent	.019	.004	.088**
Caregiver	.054*	.002	.329***
Dependence			
Parent	.069*	.008	.000
Caregiver	.022	.041**	.021
Sociability			
Parent	.025	.007	.050*
Caregiver	.087**	.001	.390***
Intelligence			
Parent	.010	.005	.009
Caregiver	.038	.016	.213***
Task orientation			
Parent	.008	.004	.000
Caregiver	.023	.012	.141***
Aggression			
Parent	.027	.015	.005
Caregiver	.002	.022	.018
Hyperactivity			
Parent	.002	.007	.027
Caregiver	.000	.028	.018
Anxiety			
Parent	.008	.011	.001
Caregiver	.056*	.060**	.081**
Peabody Picture Vocabulary Test	.063*	.001	.033*
Preschool Language Assessment Instrument	.072**	.005	.048**
Adaptive Language Inventory	.021	.021	.164***
Communication task[a]	.105		.203**

Notes. ECERS = Early Childhood Environment Rating Scale.
Age at entry was entered prior to the two family background measures.
For the social development measures, $N = 156$ for the parent ratings and 153 for the caregiver ratings.
For the PPVT-r and PLAI, $N = 131$.
For the ALI, $N = 124$.
For the Communication Task, $N = 46$.

[a] Given the small N for the communication task, a modified regression model that eliminated the two experience variables was used.

* $p < .05$. ** $p < .01$. *** $p < .001$.

The program's overall quality score was most highly associated with directors' experience.

Results

Descriptive statistics

Wide variation characterized each measure of quality. Scores on the Early Childhood Environment Rating Scale (ECERS) ranged from 66.5 to 191 ($M = 123.2$) on the 37 (low) to 259 (high) scale. Similarly, director's experience ranged from 11.3 to 24.5 years ($M = 15.7$); staff-child ratios ranged from 1:5.7 to 1:15 ($M = 1$ to 10.5 children); 1-year turnover rates ranged from 0% to 100% of the staff ($M = 39\%$); and the number of utterances spoken to children by caregivers per 10-minute observation ranged from 4.4 to 27.1 ($M = 15.6$). Furthermore, the age at entry into child care ranged from 3 to 42 months ($M = 19.2$ months), and the total time in child care ranged from 108 to 2,700 hours ($M = 1,104$ hours).

Effects of overall quality

As has been reported elsewhere (McCartney, 1984; Phillips, McCartney, & Scarr, 1987), the overall quality of the child care environment made a significant contribution to children's social and language development. Table 3-1 presents the change in R^2 at each step of the regression analysis.

With respect to social development, parents rated children in higher quality child care centers as relatively more considerate and sociable. The caregivers confirmed these two parent ratings and also indicated that children in higher quality care were more intelligent, more task oriented, and more anxious. This positive relation between quality care and anxiety is perplexing, and may be the result of a curvilinear relationship between these two variables. The centers with the highest and lowest quality ratings had equally high caregiver ratings of child anxiety. It is also important to note that the actual range of anxiety scores obtained on this sample (1.00 to 2.67) is well within the normal range on the Preschool Behavior Questionnaire on which a score at 6.73 is considered problematic (Behar, 1977). In general, the measures of social competence were more sensitive to differences in center quality than were the measures of social adjustment, and the caregiver ratings were far more predictive than the parent ratings.

The language measures also revealed a consistently positive contribution of overall program quality to child development. Quality, as measured by the ECERS, was predictive of verbal intellectual functioning assessed by the PPVT-r and of each of the three measures of language development. The two measures that involved experimenter ratings—the ALI and the communication task—were more sensitive to differences in quality than

The overall quality of the child care environment made a significant contribution to children's social and language development.

were the two standardized tests. This suggests that quality affects not only test-taking skills but also children's demonstrated communication skills.

Prior to examining the influence of program quality, the measures of family environment and child care experience yielded several significant results. Of these two sets of variables, family environment played the more predictive role. Children from homes that placed a high value on conformity were rated by their parents as more dependent and by their caregivers as less considerate, sociable, and anxious. They also performed less well on the PPVT-r, the PLAI, and the communication task. In contrast, children from homes that placed a high value on social skills were rated by their caregivers as more sociable.

Age at entry and time in care were relatively poor predictors of the children's development in child care, producing no effects on the measures of verbal intelligence and language development and only two significant relations on the social measures. Caregivers rated children who spent less time in child care as more dependent and more anxious, and children who entered care at an earlier age as more anxious.

In sum, overall quality of the child care program attended by the children in the study was positively associated with children's social and language development. This is particularly noteworthy in light of the fact that the effects of the children's age, family environment, and child care experience were controlled prior to assessing the contribution of program quality. Family background typically accounted for smaller increments in the total variance than did program quality; child care experience showed only modest effects.

Effects of specific indicators of program quality

While the finding that overall center quality is related to children's development is theoretically significant, it cannot guide practical or policy efforts to influence specific program characteristics that predict positive developmental outcomes. "What aspects of quality affect child development?" is the question that will give direction for action. In order to find some specific answers, we used the same basic regression model employed for the analyses of overall quality, but substituted four specific quality indicators in the final step: director experience, staff-child ratio, staff turnover, and verbal interactions between caregivers and children.

As a first step, however, we examined relations among these four indicators and the overall ECERS score. As can be seen in Table 3-2, we have selected relatively independent measures of program quality. The overall quality score was most highly associated with directors' experi-

Table 3-2. Correlations Among Measures of Child Care Quality

Measure	ECERS	Directors' experience	Staff-child ratio	Caregiver turnover
Directors' experience	.46			
Staff-child ratio	−.04	−.20		
Caregiver turnover	−.39	−.72	−.29	
Verbal interaction with caregivers	.30	.22	.00	−.46

Note. N = 9 centers

ence, such that programs with more experienced directors received higher ECERS scores. Higher quality programs were also associated with greater verbal interaction between caregivers and children as well as *lower* rates of caregiver turnover. The correlations among the specific quality indicators reveal that higher turnover characterized programs with less experienced directors and lower amounts of verbal interaction.

In the regression analyses, distinct patterns of influence emerged for different quality indicators (see Table 3-3). For the social measures, the director's experience and the amount of verbal interaction between caregivers and children were the most consistent predictors of development. Director experience appears to have a negative effect on children's social competence, but a positive effect on their social adjustment. Specifically, children in centers directed by more experienced adults were rated by their caregivers as less considerate and sociable, but also as less dependent, aggressive, hyperactive, and anxious. Verbal interaction, by comparison, showed consistently positive effects on parent and caregiver ratings of considerateness, and on caregiver ratings of sociability, intelligence, and task orientation.

Staff-child ratios and turnover showed a more modest degree of influence. Children in programs with fewer children per staff were rated by their parents as more considerate, but were rated by their caregivers as more anxious. Lower rates of staff turnover corresponded to lower caregiver ratings of children's dependence, sociability, and anxiety.

The children's performance on the measures of intellectual and language development were influenced primarily by staff-child ratios and amount and quality of caregiver-child verbal interaction. Children in programs with better staff-child ratios received higher scores on the PLAI, ALI, and communication assessments. Similarly, higher levels of verbal interaction corresponded to better performance on the ALI and communication assessments. No significant effects were found for director

Table 3-3. Hierarchical Regressions of Children's Social Development on Age, Family Background, Child Care Experience, and Four Specific Quality Indicators

	Change in R^2			
Measure	Director experience	Staff-child ratio	Caregiver turnover	Verbal interaction with caregiver
Considerateness				
Parent	.003	.038*	.000	.047*
Caregiver	.097**	.002	.000	.355***
Dependence				
Parent	.001	.003	.000	.012
Caregiver	.263***	.005	.156***	.009
Sociability				
Parent	.001	.021	.007	.028
Caregiver	.181***	.009	.043*	.222***
Intelligence				
Parent	.023	.002	.022	.016
Caregiver	.011	.016	.000	.234***
Task orientation				
Parent	.008	.001	.005	.001
Caregiver	.001	.001	.010	.279***
Aggression				
Parent	.009	.002	.002	.005
Caregiver	.037*	.018	.001	.000
Hyperactivity				
Parent	.000	.008	.001	.021
Caregiver	.041*	.004	.011	.005
Anxiety				
Parent	.005	.003	.003	.029
Caregiver	.056**	.130***	.052*	.002
Peabody Picture Vocabulary Test	.008	.027	.032*	.021
Preschool language Assessment Instrument	.001	.035*	.025*	.018
Adaptive Language Inventory	.000	.054**	.000	.190***
Communication task	.004	.108*	.000	.153**

Note. Each of the four quality variables was entered as the last step in four separate, but parallel, hierarchical multiple regression equations. The following variables were entered prior to this step: 1) age at testing, 2) values conformity and values social skills, 3) age at entry and time in group care.
* $p < .05$. ** $p < .01$. *** $p < .001$.

Children clearly profit from a verbally stimulating environment in which adults frequently talk with children.

---

experience for these outcome measures, and staff turnover accounted for only a modest influence; thus, children in programs with higher turnover rates received higher scores on the PPVT-r and PLAI assessments.

In sum, the amount of verbal interaction directed to children by their caregivers emerged as the strongest predictor of positive child outcomes in child care. This was true of both social and language development, with the amount of variance in these measures attributable to verbal interaction ranging from 15% to 36%, after the influences of the child's age, family environment, and child care experience were removed. The next most powerful predictor of children's social development was director experience, although its contribution was mixed. For verbal intelligence and language development, staff-child ratio showed the second strongest degree of influence. Caregiver turnover showed mixed, and relatively weak, effects indicating a negative influence on social development, but a positive influence on the PPVT-r and PLAI measures of language development.

Discussion

These results provide solid evidence of the substantial contribution that program quality makes to the development of children in child care. The influence of quality was found using analyses that included important controls for the effects of the children's age, family environment, and child care experience. The convergence of these findings with prior analyses of the Bermuda centers that compared the highest quality government-run center with the lower quality private centers (McCartney, Scarr, Phillips, & Grajek, 1985) and with the reports of other investigators (Howes, this volume; Ruopp et al., 1979; Vandell & Powers, 1983) makes a strong case for the developmental value of investing in good quality child care, not just *any* child care.

It is particularly significant that these results have emerged from research that examines representative child care centers. These results also highlight the need to examine variation in quality in all studies of child care, rather than to revert to outdated research designs in which child care is treated as a uniform intervention.

What aspects of program quality affect child development? Children clearly profit from a verbally stimulating environment in which adults frequently talk with children. This dynamic measure of quality showed the most consistently positive effects on the entire range of developmental

Higher child care standards will positively affect the development of children. Specific features of good programs are amenable to regulation and parents can observe these features when selecting child care.

outcomes; thus structural program features exert their influence through the amount of verbal interaction they encourage in the environment.

The remaining structural measures of quality — director experience, staff-child ratio, and caregiver turnover — generally made smaller contributions to the child outcomes, and in some cases showed a mixed pattern of influence. Director experience, for example, showed a negative relation to some aspects of children's social development but was also associated with better adjustment among children.

These inconsistent patterns of influence warrant further study. Certain domains of development may be differentially sensitive to certain aspects of program quality. In the present study, a strong association between director experience and social development stood alongside the lack of association between director experience and language development.

More refined measures of *experience* are also needed. The results of the National Day Care Study (Ruopp et al., 1979) revealed that caregivers — not directors — with more years of experience engaged in less social interaction and cognitive stimulation with infants and toddlers. On the other hand, Howes (1983) found that more experienced caregivers were more responsive to children's bids for attention. Clearly, not all experience is alike. That which is acquired in the context of careful supervision would not be expected to show similar effects as that acquired in a poor quality program with minimal supervision.

Research examining more complex relations among quality indicators is also needed. Interactive, compensatory, and additive influences warrant study. Good ratios, for example, may be more important in programs with less skilled caregivers than in programs with well-trained, stable caregivers. The influence of turnover rates may vary with the ability of the program director to orient new staff, or with the quality of the staff who leave versus those who remain with the program. Curvilinear relations may also emerge, such that some experience is better than none, but too much experience produces burnout. Exposure effects that entail examining interactions between program quality and time in care also deserve empirical attention because so many families rely on long-term child care.

In conclusion, good quality care is good for children. This is not a particularly astonishing result, yet it is one that has been largely ignored by researchers and policymakers. Issues of program quality are generally sidestepped in debates that emphasize the dual needs to expand the supply of child care and to make child care more affordable (Phillips, 1984). To the extent that quality is regulated, states enforce a floor below which children's health and safety are presumed to be jeopardized. This is

The amount of verbal interaction directed to children by their caregivers emerged as the strongest predictor of positive child outcomes in child care.

a far cry from efforts to assure healthy development. The research evidence from Bermuda suggests that higher child care standards will positively affect the development of children. Specific features of good programs are amenable to regulation and parents can observe these features when selecting child care.

References

Behar, L. (1977). The Preschool Behavior Questionnaire. *Journal of Abnormal Child Psychology, 5,* 265–275.
Behar, L., & Stringfield, S.A. (1974). A behavior rating scale for the preschool child. *Developmental Psychology, 10,* 601–610.
Belsky, J., Steinberg, L., & Walker, A. (1982). The ecology of daycare. In M. Lamb (Ed.), *Childrearing in nontraditional families* (pp. 71–116). Hillsdale, NJ: Erlbaum.
Blank, M., Rose, S.A., & Berlin, L.J. (1978). *PLAI: The language of learning in practice.* New York: Grune & Stratton.
Clarke-Stewart, A., & Fein, G.G. (1983). Early childhood programs. In P.H. Mussen (Series Ed.); M. Haith & J. Campos (Vol. Eds.), *Handbook of child psychology: Vol. II. Infancy and developmental psychobiology* (pp. 917–1000). New York: Wiley.
Dunn, L.M. (1979). *Peabody Picture Vocabulary Test—revised.* Circle Pines, MN: American Guidance Service.
Feagans, L., & Farran, D. (1979). *Adaptive language inventory.* Unpublished manuscript, University of North Carolina at Chapel Hill.
Harms, T., & Clifford, R.M. (1980). *Early Childhood Environment Rating Scale.* New York: Teachers College Press, Columbia University.
Howes, C. (1983). Caregiver behavior in center and family day care. *Journal of Applied Developmental Psychology, 4,* 99–107.
Howes, C., & Olenick, M. (1986). Family and child care influences on toddlers' compliance. *Child Development, 57,* 202–216.
McCartney, K. (1984). The effect of quality of day care environment upon children's language development. *Developmental Psychology, 20,* 244–260.
McCartney, K., Scarr, S., Phillips, D., & Grajek, S. (1985). Day care as intervention: Comparisons of varying quality programs. *Journal of Applied Developmental Psychology, 6,* 247–260.
Phillips, D. (1984). Day care: Promoting collaboration between research and policymaking. *Journal of Applied Developmental Psychology, 5,* 91–113.
Phillips, D., McCartney, K., & Scarr, S. (1987). Child care quality and children's social development. *Developmental Psychology, 23,* 537–543.
Prescott, E., Kritchevsky, S., & Jones, K. (1972). *The Day Care Environment Inventory.* Washington, DC: U.S. Department of Health, Education and Welfare.
Ruopp, R., Travers, J., Glantz, F., & Coelen, C. (1979). *Children at the center: Final results of the National Day Care Study.* Cambridge, MA: Abt Associates.

Schaefer, E., & Edgerton, M.D. (1977). *Parent as educator interview.* Unpublished manuscript, University of North Carolina at Chapel Hill.

Schaefer, E., & Edgerton, M.D. (1978, August). *A method and a model for describing competence and adjustment: A preschool version of the Classroom Behavior Inventory.* Paper presented at the Annual Meeting of the American Psychological Association, Toronto, Canada. (ERIC Document Reproduction Service No. ED 183 262)

Vandell, D.L., & Powers, C.P. (1983). Day care quality and children's free play activities. *American Journal of Orthopsychiatry, 53,* 493–500.

Chapter 4

Child Care Quality, Compliance With Regulations, and Children's Development: The Pennsylvania Study

Susan Kontos and Richard Fiene

THE ONLY PUBLIC POLICY designed to maintain quality control in child care consists of each state's licensing regulations. It is assumed that when child care programs comply with licensing regulations, they meet a level of quality that will, at the very least, not be harmful to the development of young children (e.g., Fiene & Nixon, 1981).

Many early childhood educators take issue with crediting the typical state child care regulatory system with anything closely related to quality. However, Morgan (1985) suggests that "Licensing establishes a basic floor of quality. A ceiling is represented by the goals of the profession" (p. 15). It is precisely this discrepancy between the floor and ceiling of quality that feeds the concern of skeptics who believe child care may be harmful for children and sparks the interest of researchers concerned about the impact of public policy on children and families.

Variation in regulatable characteristics of child care is related to differences in children's intellectual, language, and social development or experiences. Little research has been done to determine how regulatable aspects of child care (those aspects of quality that enter into licensing criteria) relate to measures of quality determined by standards of the child care profession. Although a portion of the Bermuda Study addressed this issue (McCartney, 1984; Phillips, Scarr, & McCartney, this volume), data also are needed from American settings if specific public policy implications are to be drawn. Specific information is needed regarding how much children's development is influenced by differences in regulatable characteristics of child care after all other relevant variables (e.g., age, SES, child care history) have been taken into account. Information of this nature will help determine which regulatable characteristics of centers are most critical to quality as it is defined by professional criteria and observed in child development outcomes.

A unique opportunity to obtain these data arose in the state of Pennsylvania, where the Office of Children, Youth and Families (OCYF) was wrestling with several related licensing issues. The first issue was one with which every state would like to deal: Pennsylvania had recently implemented an instrument-based program monitoring system to determine the level of center compliance to licensing regulations. The average center in the state was in compliance with 97% of the regulations (Fiene, 1980). Most centers, therefore, met the basic floor of quality.

Second, child care centers in Pennsylvania are required to apply to and be accepted by the state as licensed vendors of subsidized child care slots. Consistent with its goal of promoting child development, OCYF wanted to know that vendors selected to provide subsidized care are providing high quality care as defined by standards in the profession and by positive child development outcomes. Because most programs complied with the licensing regulations, however, the state had no way to objectively discriminate among the quality of services provided by centers. Thus, OCYF sought data to help pinpoint key quality indicators from individual regulatable center characteristics by determining how well these characteristics predict child development outcomes, licensing compliance scores, and an environmental quality score as defined by early childhood professionals. OCYF planned to translate the knowledge obtained from these data into public policy concerning child care regulation and funding. The study described here was conducted in collaboration with OCYF.

Conducting the study

Centers

The 10 centers that participated in the study were randomly selected from a sample of 25 centers that volunteered. Those 25 were part of a sample of 40 centers selected as representative of the 350 centers in the northeast region of Pennsylvania (i.e., half urban, half with enrollment more than 30, half nonprofit). The random sample of 10 participating centers was stratified to approximate the proportion of urban/rural and profit/nonprofit centers in that region of the state. Thus, of the 10 centers, five were urban/nonprofit, three were urban/profit, and one each was rural/nonprofit and rural/profit.

Children and parents

Child care directors provided a list of all 3-, 4-, and 5-year-old children who had attended the center full-time (more than 20 hours per week) for at least 6 months. Of these, 100 randomly selected children participated. These 100 children were divided by gender (53 males and 47 females), were predominantly White, and were from all socioeconomic levels. Children's mean age was 53 months. Their average age of entry into out of home care was 24.98 months, and the average time spent in child care was 4,084 hours. Mean annual family income was $26,512 with a range of no income to $100,000. Mothers whose children participated agreed to be interviewed by the researcher by telephone. See Table 4-1 for further descriptions of the sample.

Table 4-1. Means, Standard Deviations, and Ranges for Each Variable

Variable	X	SD	Range
Age of child (months)	52.80	8.66	36–70
Family background			
Mother's education (years)	13.07	2.74	4–21
Value for prosocial (score)	10.28	2.24	5–14
Child care experience			
Age at child care entry (months)	24.98	14.64	1–60
Time in care (hours)	4084.43	2097.14	270–9360
Center quality			
ECERS	139.62	21.59	111–176
CDPE-IC (%)	88.94	7.03	80–100
CDPE	34.00	39.48	−51–100
COFAS	67.97	10.54	54–87
Center characteristics			
Turnover (%)	27.88	19.99	0–70
Capacity	66.16	33.33	20–127
Group size	22.85	6.67	15–39
Ratio	9.81	2.06	6–15
Director's experience (years)	8.09	3.88	2–14
Average staff experience (years)	6.51	3.88	24–145
4-year degree (%)	49.00	56.00	0–100
Child development outcomes			
Slosson	112.47	16.84	71–150
CBI-Int	52.83	18.34	−5–91
TELD	101.72	13.07	67–130
ALI	60.29	11.41	33–90
PBQ	15.91	9.60	0–38
CBI-Soc	31.89	14.48	2–67

Family background is the most salient determinant of development in children attending child care centers whose quality varies from adequate to good.

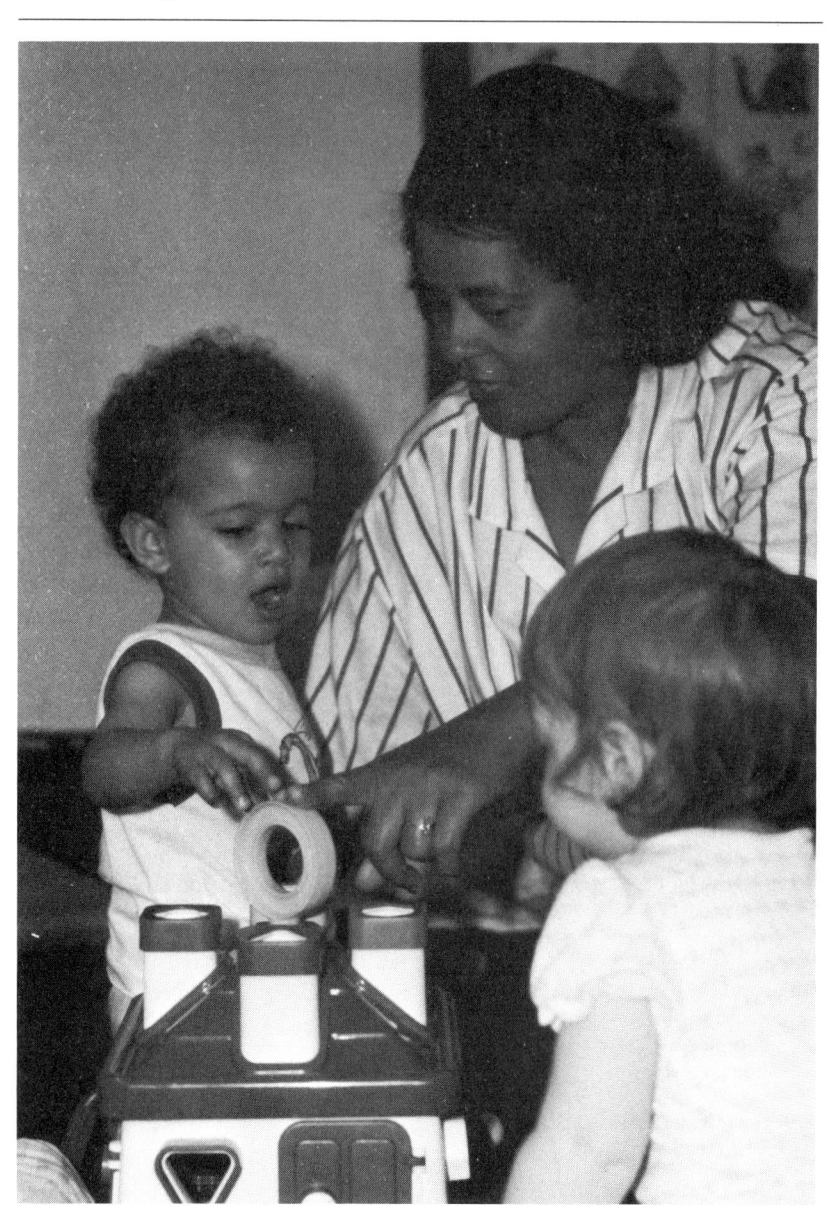

Measures of center quality
Four measures of center quality were administered for each center. Three of these measures were scales developed by the Pennsylvania Office of Children, Youth and Families in order to determine whether a center qualifies for fully or provisionally licensed status — the Child Development Program Evaluation Scale (CDPE) (Fiene, Douglas, & Kroh, 1978), the CDPE Indicator Checklist (CDPE-IC) (Fiene, 1984), and the Caregiver Observation Form and Scale (COFAS) (Fiene, 1984). These were the *floor of quality* measures. The fourth measure was a more comprehensive measure of overall environmental quality — the Early Childhood Environment Rating Scale (ECERS) (Harms & Clifford, 1980). This measure represents professional goals for quality. The CDPE and the CDPE-IC measure structural variables in child care. The COFAS and a significant portion of the ECERS measure process variables.

Compliance with licensing regulations in Pennsylvania is monitored through an instrument-based system. Each regulation has been translated into a dichotomous item with stated criteria that determine whether or not a center is in compliance with that regulation. Those items together form a 270-item instrument, known as the Child Development Program Evaluation (CDPE), that is administered annually by a regional licensing representative from the state during a lengthy site visit. The CDPE is comprised of the following seven subscales: program administration, environmental safety, child development program and curriculum, health, nutrition, parent involvement, and transportation.

Each item on the CDPE was empirically given a weight (translated into points) based on ratings of the level of risk to children's health and safety if the center is out of compliance (see Fiene & Nixon, 1981, for method of determining weights). Centers begin with a perfect total score of 100, and points are then subtracted when a center is out of compliance on a particular item. For this study, the CDPE total score on file for each center from the last site visit was one of three measures of quality related to compliance to licensing regulations.

The second measure of quality involving compliance to licensing regulations was the percent of items passed on the CDPE Indicator Checklist (CDPE-IC). The CDPE-IC is a 15-item scale comprised of the best predictors of the total score from the full scale (Fiene & Nixon, 1985). Items focus on staff ratios and qualifications, environmental safety, supervision, presence of health appraisals on children and staff, emergency contacts for children, food preparation, use of safety carriers during transportation, and social service agreement forms. An additional item based on an observation of caregiver behavior comprised a separate scale (COFAS) in the present study and is described below. The CDPE-IC was administered at each center by a regional licensing representative and a child care center director (from a different center) shortly after the children's data were obtained. Both people administered both the CDPE-IC and the COFAS simultaneously but independently and reached a consensus on any items about which there was disagreement.

The observation of caregiver behavior (COFAS) is designed to determine if adult behavior in the child care setting promotes development of skills, self-esteem, and positive self-identity and provides for a choice of activities. The COFAS (Fiene, 1984) is a list of 29 caregiver behaviors that are coded during a 20-minute classroom observation, assigned their designated weight, and summed for a total score. A score of 30 or above is required for the caregiver to be in compliance with the observation item on the Indicator Checklist. Items comprising the COFAS were selected following extensive field testing (see Fiene & Nixon, 1981).

The Early Childhood Environment Rating Scale (ECERS) (Harms & Clifford, 1980) was administered at each center by one of the three-member research team. This scale consists of 37 items judged by early childhood professionals to be extremely important components of quality programs for children and has been shown to have high interrater reliability (McCartney, 1984; Harms & Clifford, 1980). The items focus on seven areas of quality (personal care routines, furnishings and display, language and reasoning experiences, creative activities, fine and gross motor activities, social development, adult needs).

Center characteristics

Seven center characteristics — one process variable and six structural variables — were individually measured: staff turnover, center capacity, staff-child ratio, group size, director's experience, average staff experience, and proportion of staff with 4-year degrees. Of these variables, only turnover was not regulatable. Staff turnover rate, the process variable, was measured by determining the proportion of staff positions that had been replaced in the previous year (or 2 years if the proportion was more representative). Only one staff member with a 4-year degree held it in a non-child-related major — psychology; the remainder of the degrees were in elementary education, early childhood education, or special education.

Children's development

Two measures each of intellectual, language, and social development were obtained for each child. Intellectual development was measured by the Slosson Intelligence Test (Slosson, 1983) and the intellectual functioning subtest of the Classroom Behavior Inventory — Preschool Form (Schaefer & Edgerton, 1978). The Slosson Intelligence Test is an individually administered test of mental ability adapted from the Stanford-Binet (Form L-M). The Classroom Behavior Inventory — Preschool Form is a 60-item rating scale of which 30 items comprise the intellectual functioning subtest. This includes five subscales with items concerning task orientation versus distractibility, creativity/curiosity versus apathy, and verbal intelligence. See Schaefer and Edgerton (1978) for details.

Language development was measured by the Test of Early Language Development (TELD) (Hresko, Reid, & Hammill, 1981) and the Adaptive Language Inventory (Feagans & Farran, 1979). The TELD, an individually administered standardized test of language development, is designed to measure two dimensions of language — form and content — in both the receptive and expressive mode. For this study, the dependent measure was the language quotient. The Adaptive Language Inventory is an 18-item teacher rating scale of children's verbal ability in a classroom setting (see D. Farran, personal communication, 1984). Items focus on comprehension, production, rephrasing, spontaneity, listening, and fluency. All Adaptive Language Inventory item scores were summed for a total score.

Social development was measured by the Preschool Behavior Questionnaire (a 30-item behavior problem checklist that assesses social deviance) (Behar & Stringfield, 1974) and the sociability subtest of the Classroom Behavior Inventory. The Preschool Behavior Questionnaire is a modification of Rutter's Children's Behavior Questionnaire (Rutter, 1967). The items describe behaviors ranging from "squirmy and fidgety" to "unusual sexual behaviors." The questionnaire was designed to help identify children with symptoms of emotional disturbance. The second measure of social development was the 30 items relating to sociability remaining on the Classroom Behavior Inventory — Preschool Form (Schaefer & Edgerton, 1978). These items form six subscales related to extroversion/introversion, considerateness/hostility, and independence/dependence.

Four of the measures of children's development are identical to some used in the Bermuda Study: the Preschool Behavior Questionnaire, the Adaptive Language Inventory, and the Classroom Behavior Inventory, which are all teacher rating scales. The Slosson Intelligence Test and the TELD are standardized tests administered by the researchers.

Family background

A standardized telephone interview was used to obtain family background information from the mother (only one mother could not be

Floor of quality appears to be different from a professional standard of quality, and the floor of quality measures appear to be somewhat different from one another.

---

reached). The interview focused on demographic characteristics of the family (age, occupation, marital status, income, family size, and education), access to a Title XX child care subsidy, the child's supplemental care history, childrearing and education values for the child (from the Parent as Educator Interview, Schaefer & Edgerton, 1979), and variety of stimulation in the home (from the HOME Inventory, Caldwell & Bradley, 1978).

In order to determine mothers' childrearing and education values, interviewers asked them to rank three sets of five statements about varying priorities for childrearing and education (Schaefer & Edgerton, 1979). The ranks were summed to form three subscores that indicated relative value for conformity, prosocial behavior, and independent problem solving in children's behavior.

The "variety of stimulation" subtest of the HOME Inventory (Caldwell & Bradley, 1978) provided a measure of home environment stimulation. Nine items concerning children's excursions away from home, participation in grocery shopping, inclusion at mealtime, the types of toys, and the display of children's artwork were scored as pass or fail. The total items passed comprised the home environment stimulation score.

Procedure

A team of three researchers visited each center for one day to obtain the ECERS scores and administer to children the Slosson Intelligence Test and the TELD. Children's primary caregivers were given instructions for completing the rating scales. They were asked to complete, the rating scales item by item for all children so that they were using comparable scoring criteria. Researchers interviewed directors at the center to obtain information concerning the center characteristics. They conducted telephone interviews with children's mothers after the center visit.

Results of the study

Quality variables

Table 4-1 presents means, standard deviations, and ranges for each variable included in the analyses. All centers were qualified for a license based on the CDPE-IC and the COFAS. According to scores on the full CDPE, only six centers qualified to be fully licensed, three could be provisionally licensed, and one would be denied a license.

The mean ECERS total score indicated that the average item score on this measure for all centers was slightly above *adequate*, but less than *good*. The average ECERS item score for the lowest scoring center was *adequate*. For the highest scoring center, the average ECERS item score was slightly below *good*.

These data suggest that the centers participating in the study represented a range of quality, both in terms of licensing criteria and in terms of professional standards. Several centers received *perfect* quality scores on the licensing measures; none of the centers scored at either extreme of quality as measured by the ECERS.

The intercorrelations among the quality variables reveal an interesting pattern (see Table 4-2). Correlations were consistently low to moderate. Predictably, the highest correlation was between the full CDPE and the CDPE-IC. In fact, because those two scores ostensibly measure the same thing, an even higher relationship was expected.

The most important of the correlations among quality variables were those between the ECERS (the professional standard for quality) and the three licensing variables (the floor of quality). Interestingly, the ECERS was most strongly related to the COFAS, the measure of caregiver behaviors. The relationship between the ECERS and the total CDPE was only slightly weaker. What is notable about these correlations is that their small to moderate strength suggests that these measures of quality overlap very little with one another. In other words, the floor of quality appears to be different from a professional standard of quality, and floor of quality measures appear to be somewhat different from one another. Another possibility is that the two aspects of quality do not have a linear relationship and thus a correlation coefficient may not be an accurate index of the relationship.

Relationships between quality measures and center characteristics

One purpose of our study was to determine how well individual characteristics of centers (most of them regulatable) predicted measures of quality, and vice versa, as defined by licensing criteria and by professional standards. Of the seven individual center characteristics, four predicted caregiver behavior (COFAS), two the total CDPE, and three ECERS. For this sample, the individual center characteristics were most strongly related to caregiver behavior both in number and strength of correlations. Capacity, group size, and ratio were the structural characteristics most consistently related to any aspect of quality. Larger center capacity and more children per caregiver predicted lower quality as measured by the ECERS (for both variables) and the CDPE-IC (for capac-

Table 4.2. Correlations Between Center Characteristics and Center Quality Measures (N = 10)

	Center characteristics							Quality measures			
	Turnover	Capacity	Group size	Ratio	Director's experience	Average staff experience	4-year degree	ECERS	CDPE-IC	CDPE	COFAS
Characteristics											
Turnover	—	.04	.47	.35	−.44	−.34	.34	.10	.01	−.02	−.66
Capacity		—	−.39	.48	−.36	−.34	.39	−.41	−.56	−.04	−.15
Group size			—	−.27	.08	−.04	−.14	.46	.44	−.23	−.18
Ratio				—	−.51	−.41	.33	−.47	−.21	−.26	−.61
Director's experience					—	.75	−.50	.32	.15	−.15	.73
Average staff experience						—	−.29	.29	.22	.002	.57
4-year degree							—	−.12	−.28	.10	−.33
Quality											
ECERS								—	.36	.28	.38
CDPE-IC									—	.44	.19
CDPE										—	.31
COFAS											—

Note: Due to sample size, no significance levels are reported.

Capacity, group size, and ratio were the structural characteristics most consistently related to any aspect of quality.

ity) or COFAS (for ratio). Interestingly, and contrary to findings in other studies, group size was positively related to quality. The strong negative relationship between staff turnover and COFAS and the strong relationship between director's experience and COFAS are noteworthy. These data suggest that structural and process components of staff characteristics are related to caregiver behavior.

Relationships with children's development

The contribution of variations in center quality and center characteristics to children's development was measured in two ways. Initially, we correlated the child development measures with the measures of center quality and of individual center characteristics using Pearson Product-Moment correlations. The results of these analyses can be seen in Table 4-3. In general, the correlations were small, but a number of them reach significance because of the sample size. Three of the correlations stand out because of their strength. Higher quality, as measured by the CDPE-IC, and smaller center capacity were related to lower social deviance scores on the Preschool Behavior Questionnaire. Less director experience in child care was related to higher TELD scores.

In general, center characteristics and quality measures most consistently predicted language development as measured by the TELD. These correlations were all negative, however, and difficult to explain. Most probably, the reason is related to a confounding of center quality with family background: The lower quality programs tended to be in profit centers where more middle-class children, who performed better on the developmental assessments, were enrolled.

Needless to say these correlations were confounded with children's ages, family background, and child care experience. The subsequent set of analyses attempted to control for the effects of these variables in order to obtain a clearer picture of how children's development is affected by individual center characteristics and center quality.

Regression analyses

Design. We used a hierarchical multiple regression model to control for the influence of children's age, family background, and child care history prior to examining the extent to which children's cognitive, language, and social development was affected by variation in individual center characteristics and center quality. A four-step process was implemented to determine predictors of children's development and to examine the influence of center characteristics. At each step, we calculated the amount of variance in children's cognitive, language, and social development accounted for by the set of predictor variables. The analysis indicated how much *additional* variance was accounted for by subsequent predictors added to the model.

A diagram of the model is presented in Figure 4-1. For the first step, children's age was the only predictor of the developmental measures. Then the three family background variables found to influence center selection were added simultaneously to form step 2. It was important to know whether centers with certain quality scores were selected by families of a

Table 4-3. Correlations of Center Characteristics and Quality Measures with Child Development Outcome Measures

	\multicolumn{6}{c}{Child development outcomes (n = 100)}
	Intellectual		Language		Social	
	Slosson	CBI-Int	TELD	ALI	PBQ	CBI-Soc
Characteristics						
Turnover	−.12	.04	−.06	.10	.16	.13
Capacity	.02	−.17	.11	−.05	.25*	−.06
Group size	−.21*	−.02	−.22*	.02	−.06	.07
Ratio	−.005	−.08	.06	−.02	.12	.12
Director's experience	−.23*	.02	−.33*	−.06	−.003	−.20*
Average staff experience	−.09	.10	−.20*	.05	−.09	.006
4-year degree	.16	.06	.18	.09	.14	.14
Quality						
ECERS	−.20*	.03	−.21*	.07	.02	−.04
CDPE-IC	−.003	.01	−.02	.03	−.39*	.21*
CDPE	.16	.03	.20*	.08	−.18	.10
COFAS	.14	−.05	−.22*	−.03	−.02	−.22*

*$p < .05$

Figure 4-1. Diagram of Multiple Regression Model

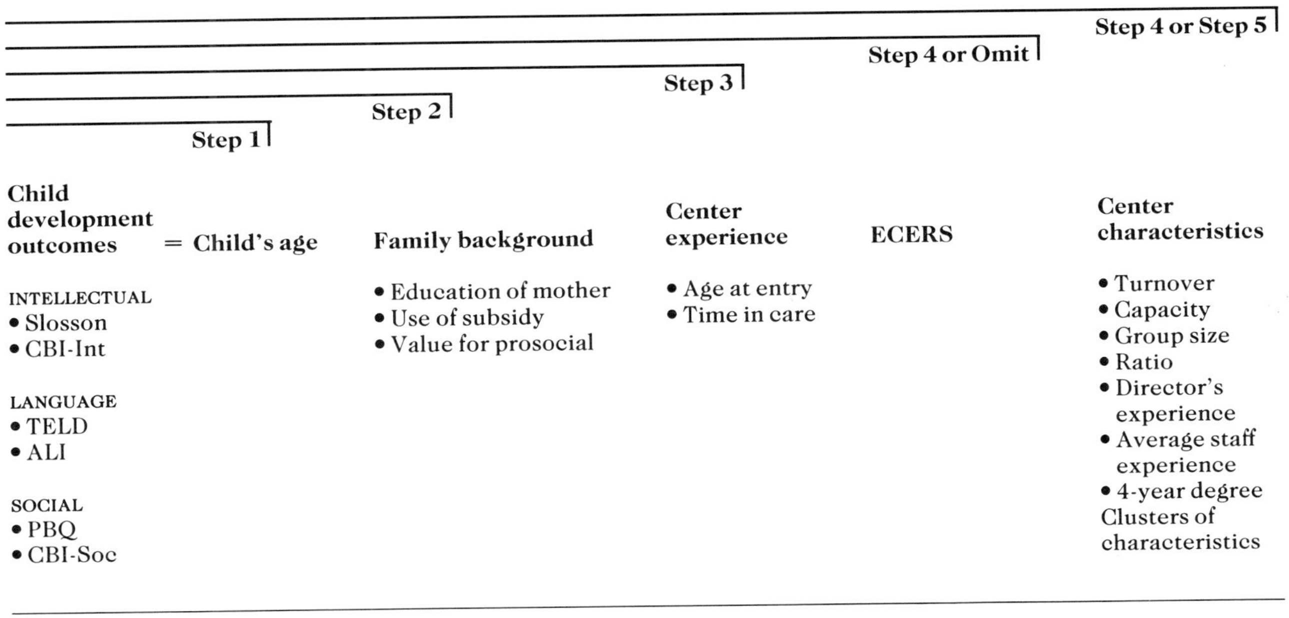

	Step 1	Step 2	Step 3	Step 4 or Omit	Step 4 or Step 5
Child development outcomes	= Child's age	Family background	Center experience	ECERS	Center characteristics
INTELLECTUAL • Slosson • CBI-Int LANGUAGE • TELD • ALI SOCIAL • PBQ • CBI-Soc		• Education of mother • Use of subsidy • Value for prosocial	• Age at entry • Time in care		• Turnover • Capacity • Group size • Ratio • Director's experience • Average staff experience • 4-year degree Clusters of characteristics

particular background. Three family variables — mother's education, use of a child care subsidy, and maternal value for prosocial behavior — predicted center quality and became control variables in the final regression analysis.

Step 3 involved adding two variables concerned with the child's supplemental care history (age at entry into group care and length of time in group care). This step estimated the effects of exposure to child care environments, regardless of their quality.

Finally, each of the seven measures of center characteristics was added to the model individually and in a cluster as step 4 to estimate the influence of center characteristics (alone and in combination) with the influence of all other variables removed. In order to minimize the confounding among the clusters of regulatable center characteristics, Pearson Product-Moment correlation coefficients were calculated among all seven characteristics. Only combinations of characteristics whose intercorrelations were below .30 were included in a cluster.

A five-step process was implemented to examine the same relationships, but with the inclusion of center quality as a predictor of children's development. Of the five steps, the first three remained the same as in the four-step process. Step four, however, involved adding one center quality variable, ECERS. This step estimated the effects of child care quality (as defined by professional standards) on children's development with the influence of all other variables removed. The fifth step involved once more adding each center characteristic individually and in clusters to the equation. The purpose of step 5 was to determine if the amount of influence accounted for by the center characteristics changed when the effects for center quality were removed first. This approach, modeled after that used in the National Day Care Study, was designed to estimate an upper and lower range for the amount of variance in child development outcomes accounted for by center characteristics with and without the variance due to center quality removed first.

Findings. Table 4-4 presents the beta weights for each variable, the *R*, and the proportion of variance added by each of the four steps for each of the six child development variables. Age was a significant predictor of development only for two nonstandardized measures, the intellectual functioning subtest of the Classroom Behavior Inventory — Preschool and the Adaptive Language Inventory. For three of the six child development measures, family background was the prime and/or only significant predictor: Slosson Intelligence (intellectual development), the TELD, and the Adaptive Language Inventory (language development). Neither mea-

Table 4-4. Results of Hierarchical Multiple Regression Analyses (Beta Weights and R^2)

			Family Background			Center Experience		Quality		
Measure	Step	Age	Mother's education	Subsidy	Value for prosocial	When entered care	Time in care	ECERS	R^2	R^2
Slosson	1	.075							.001	
	2	.144	1.29*						.13*	.129*
	3	.418	1.15	5.54	1.37	−.384*	−.0009		.185*	.055
	4	.40	1.26*	4.17	1.43*	−.394*	−.001	.085	.193*	.008
				1.76	1.31					
CBI-Int	1	−.55*							.067	
	2	.63*	1.46						.145	.078
	3	.72*	1.41	−2.7	.62	−.12	−.0003		.149*	.004
	4	.72*	1.41*	−3.12	.64	−.12	−.0003	.0015	.150*	.001
				−3.08	.64					
TELD	1	−.04							.0007	
	2	.05	.73						.155*	.15*
	3	.20	.66	4.81	1.52*	−.198	−.0008		.176*	.02
	4	.19	.72	4.26	1.55*	−.204	−.0008	−.049	.179*	.003
				2.86	1.48*					
ALI	1	.37*							.08	
	2	.39*	.84*						.188*	.111*
	3	.44*	.82*	−4.34*	.97*	−.06	−.0004		.19*	.002
	4	.44*	.82*	−4.43*	.98*	−.06	−.0003	−.006	.19*	.00
				−4.61	.97*					
PBQ	1	−.07							.004	
	2	−.09	.89*						.09	.086
	3	.03	.94	−1.24	.33	−.15	−.0007		.1119	.02
	4	.02	.88	−1.57	−.03	−.15	−.0008	−.047	.1119	.00
				−2.92	−.37					
CBI-Soc	1	.23							.02	
	2	.29	1.03*						.08	.06
	3	.21	1.07*	.86	.78	.10	.0005		.008	.008
	4	.21	1.04	1.10	.76	.10	.0004	.02	.09	.002
				1.77	.80					

*$p < .05$

sure of social development was affected by variation in family background. Child care history failed to account for a significant portion of the variance for any of the six child development variables. Of the control variables included in steps 1 through 3, family background proved to be an important factor.

Of crucial importance to the purpose of the study was the effect of center quality on children's development after the effects of the control variables were removed. It is particularly significant, then, that when ECERS was entered as step 4, it accounted for none or next to none of the variance in children's development on *any* of the measures. In this study, center quality as defined by professional standards did not predict children's development when age, family background, and child care history were taken into account.

Of equal importance to the purpose of the study was the effect of center characteristics, alone and in combination, on children's development. Table 4-5 reports the proportion of variance accounted for by each center characteristic entered alone at step 4, without ECERS, and alone at step 5, after ECERS, on children's development. The proportions of variance in children's development accounted for by individual center characteristics ranged from 0 to .07 and were similar at step 4 and step 5 due to the lack of effects for ECERS. Center capacity contributed 6.8 to 7% and staff turnover contributed 2.7 to 4.2% of the variance for social deviance. Group size contributed 3.6 to 3.8% of the variance for language development (TELD) and 2.3 to 3% of the variance for intellectual development (Slosson). Staff turnover contributed 2.9 to 3.5% of the variance for intellectual development (Slosson).

The remaining proportions of variance accounted for by center characteristics were smaller. In nearly every instance, the effects of center characteristics were greater than the effects of quality on children's development. The fact remains that the effects of all the individual center characteristics on children's development were statistically nonsignificant.

Table 4-6 reports the proportion of variance accounted for by clusters of center characteristics entered at step 4, without ECERS, and at step 5, after ECERS. These results revealed two statistically significant effects, both of them involving the sociability subtest of the Classroom Behavior Inventory—Preschool. Two statistically significant effects would be expected solely due to chance. Director experience and average staff experience together contributed 16.2 to 16.4% of the variance for sociability. Those two variables combined with group size contributed 18.8 to

Table 4-5. Proportion of Variance Accounting for Child Development Outcomes by Each Center Characteristic

	Slosson		CBI-Int		TELD		ALI		PBQ		CBI-Soc	
	Step 4	Step 5	Step 4	Step 5	Step 4	Step 5	Step 4	Step 5	Step 4	Step 5	Step 4	Step 5
Turnover	.035	.029	.001	0	.024	.021	.007	.008	.027	.042	.011	.011
Capacity	.0009	.037	.021	.027	.01	.008	.002	.002	.068	.07	.0002	.001
Group size	.03	.023	.019	0	.038	.036	0	0	.008	.01	.007	.007
Ratio	.021	.037	.021	.025	.004	.011	.005	.006	.046	.046	.002	.005
Director's experience	.001	0	.01	.009	.019	.018	0	0	.015	.018	.018	.021
Average staff experience	.009	.019	0	.08	.003	0	.004	.04	.005	.057	0	.025
4-year degree	.003	.025	.001	.009	.001	.027	0	.011	.003	.02	.004	.029

Table 4-6. Proportion of Variance Accounting for Child Development Outcomes by Clusters of Center Characteristics

	Slosson		CBI-Int		TELD		ALI		PBQ		CBI-Soc	
	Step 4	Step 5	Step 4	Step 5	Step 4	Step 5	Step 4	Step 5	Step 4	Step 5	Step 4	Step 5
Turnover-Capacity	.035	.027	.023	.028	.036	.034	.008	.011	.091	.091	.014	.014
Ratio-Group size	.065	.064	.024	.025	.051	.049	.005	.006	.047	.048	.013	.012
Group size-Director's experience	.031	.023	.01	.009	.054	.055	.002	.002	.023	.024	.025	.024
Group size-Average staff experience	.043	.035	.082	.083	.038	.037	.044	.045	.066	.066	.037	.038
Group size-4-year degree	.051	.043	.01	.009	.056	.056	.011	.011	.022	.023	.04	.039
Director's experience-Average staff experience	.047	.046	.109	.109	.039	.038	.109	.109	.057	.062	.162*	.164*
Average staff experience-4-year degree	.074	.069	.13	.129	.033	.031	.081	.081	.055	.058	.084	.087
Group size-Director's experience-Average staff experience	.066	.058	.111	.112	.068	.064	.112	.113	.073	.074	.188*	.189*
Group Size-Average staff experience-4-year degree	.085	.077	.136	.135	.057	.056	.085	.085	.066	.061	.112	.112

*$p < .05$

18.9% of the variance for sociability. Seven additional effects of greater than 10% approached significance. Four of these involved the intellectual functioning subtest of the Classroom Behavior Inventory — Preschool and two involved the Adaptive Language Inventory. Treating center characteristics as clusters produced noticeably stronger effects on measures of children's development than treating them singly.

Several combinations of center characteristics contributed substantially, though not significantly, to children's development. Director experience and average staff experience (10.9% of the variance); average staff experience and proportion of 4-year degrees (12.9 to 13% of the variance); group size combined with director experience and average staff experience (11.1 to 11.2% of the variance); and group size combined with average staff experience and proportion of 4-year degrees (13.5 to 13.6% of the variance) all contributed noticeably to the variance in children's intellectual development as measured by the Classroom Behavior Inventory — Preschool. Group size, director experience, and average staff experience contributed 11.2 to 11.3% of the variance in language development as measured by the Adaptive Language Inventory. Director experience and average staff experience contributed 10.9% of the variance to that measure of language development. Finally, group size, average staff experience, and proportion of 4-year degrees contributed 11.2% of the variance in sociability. In general, clusters of center characteristics had the strongest effects (>10% of the variance accounted for) on the intellectual functioning and sociability subtests of the Classroom Behavior Inventory — Preschool and on the Adaptive Language Inventory, all teacher rating scales.

Discussion

The results suggest that family background is the most salient determinant of development in children attending day care centers whose quality varies from adequate to good. The strength of family background as a predictor in and of itself ought not to come as a total surprise. These results are consistent with a major study of public school quality and children's cognitive development and educational attainment (Jencks, 1972). In that study family background explained half of the variance in children's educational attainment while school quality added little or nothing to predictions of cognitive development or educational attainment.

The lack of statistically significant effects for individual center characteristics on children's development is certainly not a

More recently, Clarke-Stewart (Clarke-Stewart, this volume; Clarke-Stewart & Gruber, 1984) found no significant correlations between forms and features of family day care homes and children's intellectual and social competence when variation due to family background variables was partialled out. To a lesser extent, this also occurred for center-based child care programs.

In the Bermuda Study, family background variables were as predictive of children's language development as child care quality (McCartney, 1984; Phillips, Scarr, & McCartney, this volume). Clearly the data regarding family background and child care quality gleaned from this study are partially consistent with other data.

Moreover, the range of quality represented must be taken into account as we draw conclusions. Center quality, as measured by the ECERS, was a significant predictor of development in the Bermuda Study, but not in this study. Why the difference? In examining the differences between the centers participating in the two studies, it is immediately clear that the Pennsylvania centers, while they varied in quality, were substantially different in the range of quality than the Bermuda centers. The lowest quality center in Pennsylvania had an average item score of adequate while in Bermuda the average item score for the low quality centers was much lower. The implication may be that when child care quality ranges from adequate to good the differential effects of quality are nonexistent. When the lower range of quality drops below adquate, the differential effects may become salient due to detrimental effects of low quality care on children's development.

This is not consistent with Vandell and Powers's (1983) data that showed medium quality centers were more like low quality than high quality centers. They were using floor of quality measures, however, not professional standards. Being at a moderate level with respect to the floor of quality may indeed have different implications for children's development than being moderate in quality using professional standards.

Looking at the individual center characteristics in isolation, we found that capacity, group size, and ratio were most frequently related to quality regardless of how it was measured. Contrary to the results of the National Day Care Study (Ruopp, 1979), however, group size was positively related to quality. On the other hand, the negative relationship between caregiver-child ratio and quality is consistent with the National Day Care Study findings. Consistent with the findings of Howes and Rubenstein (1985) and Vandell and Powers (1983), staff characteristics (turnover, ratio, director's experience, and average staff experience) predicted caregiver behavior (as *sign that policymakers are free to deregulate child care without fear of harming children.*

measured by the COFAS). Children's performances on the Slosson Intelligence Test and TELD were the child development outcome variables most frequently related to individual center characteristics, particularly group size and director's experience. Recall that earlier these negative correlations were explained by confounding between center quality, profit status, and children's performance on developmental measures.

The results clearly show that individual center characteristics were much more powerful as predictors of children's development when they were treated in clusters than alone. The clusters of characteristics explained more than 10% of the variance in several measures of development and in two instances explained between 15 to 20% of the variance. The latter two were statistically significant predictors.

The lack of statistically significant effects for individual center characteristics (alone or in clusters) on children's development is certainly not a sign that policymakers are free to deregulate child care without fear of harming children. These results are a function of the characteristics of a small sample of 10 centers. The *typical* range of regulated center characteristics in Pennsylvania or any other state is unknown. Another line of reasoning suggests that researchers have yet to determine at what point an effect can be said to have a substantive impact on development, even when it is statistically significant. A number of effects that approached significance suggest that this study warrants replication in order to draw firmer conclusions regarding how structural and process characteristics of child care centers affect children's development.

With the added perspective of previous research, one thing that these data tell us is how far we have to go in understanding how variations in child care environments affect children's development. Consistencies and inconsistencies between studies ought to remind us of the innumerable variables that may be acting as a smoke screen to, rather than shedding light on, the relationship between child care quality and children's development. For instance, state-to-state variations in licensing regulations and monitoring, demographic variables related to families and communities, when and in what country the study was conducted, size of the sample of centers, and type of child development outcome measures are factors that singly and together surely influence the results of research in this area. This study contributes to the knowledge base by showing how, within the confines of the measures used and the sample of families and centers, family background contributes more to variation in children's development than center quality or individual center characteristics.

References

Behar, L., & Stringfield, S. (1974). A behavior rating scale for the preschool child. *Developmental Psychology, 10,* 601–610.

Caldwell, B., & Bradley, R. (1978). *Home Observation for Measurement of the Environment: Administration Manual.* Little Rock, AR: University of Arkansas.

Clarke-Stewart, K.A., & Gruber, C. (1984). Day care forms and features. In R. Ainslie (Ed.), *The child and the day care setting: Qualitative variations and development* (pp. 35–62). New York: Praeger.

Feagans, L., & Farran, D. (1979). Adaptive Language Inventory. Unpublished instrument. University of North Carolina, Chapel Hill.

Fiene, R. (1980, September). State day care program compliance with state regulations. Unpublished manuscript. Office of Children, Youth and Families, Harrisburg, PA.

Fiene, R. (1984). *Child Development Program Evaluation Scale and COFAS.* Washington, DC: Children's Services Monitoring Consortium.

Fiene, R., Douglas, E., & Kroh, K. (1978, January). Center licensing instrument. Unpublished manuscript. Office of Children, Youth and Families, Harrisburg, PA.

Fiene, R., & Nixon, M. (1981). *Instrument-based program monitoring information systems series.* Washington, DC: Children's Services Monitoring Consortium.

Fiene, R., & Nixon, M. (1985). Instrument-based program monitoring and the indicator checklist for child care. *Child Care Quarterly, 14,* 28–46.

Harms, T., & Clifford, R. (1980). *Early Childhood Environment Rating Scale.* New York: Teachers College Press, Columbia University.

Howes, C., & Rubenstein, J. (1985). Determinants of toddlers' experience in daycare: Age of entry and quality of setting. *Child Care Quarterly, 14,* 140, 151.

Hresko, W., Reid, D.K., & Hammill, P.D. (1981). *The Test of Early Language Development.* Austin, TX: Pro-Ed.

Jencks, C. (1972). *Inequality: A reassessment of the effect of family and schooling in America.* New York: Basic.

McCartney, K. (1984). Effect of quality of day care environment on children's language development. *Developmental Psychology, 20,* 244–260.

Morgan, G. (1985). The government perspective. In G. Morgan, N. Curry, R. Endsley, M. Bradbard, H. Rashid, & A. Epstein (Eds.), *Quality in early childhood programs: Four perspectives.* (High/Scope Early Childhood Policy Papers, No. 3) Ypsilanti, MI: High/Scope.

Ruopp, R. (1979). *Children at the center: Final report of the National Day Care Study. Executive summary.* Cambridge, MA: Abt Associates.

Rutter, M. (1967). A children's behavior questionnaire for completion by teachers: Preliminary findings. *Journal of Child Psychology and Psychiatry, 8,* 1–11.

Schaefer, E., & Edgerton, M. (1978, August). *A method and a model for describing competence and adjustment: A preschool version of the Classroom Behavior Inventory.* Paper presented at the Annual Meeting of the American Psychological Association, Toronto, Canada. (ERIC Document Reproduction Service No. ED 183 262)

Schaefer, E., & Edgerton, M. (1979). Parent as educator interview—short form. Unpublished manuscript, University of North Carolina, Chapel Hill.

Slosson, R. (1983). *Slosson Intelligence Test.* Slosson Educational Publications. P.O. Box 280, East Aurora, NY 14052.

Vandell, D.L., & Powers, C. (1983). Day care quality and children's free play activities. *American Journal of Orthopsychiatry, 53,* 493–500.

This study was funded by a Research Initiation Grant from the Pennsylvania State University when the first author was on the faculty there. Appreciation is expressed to Irene Molzahn, the Northeast Regional Licensing representatives, and the staff and families of the participating centers. Cathy Thompson and Marie Bellows deserve special thanks for their work as research assistants.

Parents observe teachers for suggestions of ways to engage with their child. Thus, trained teachers engage in informal parent education.

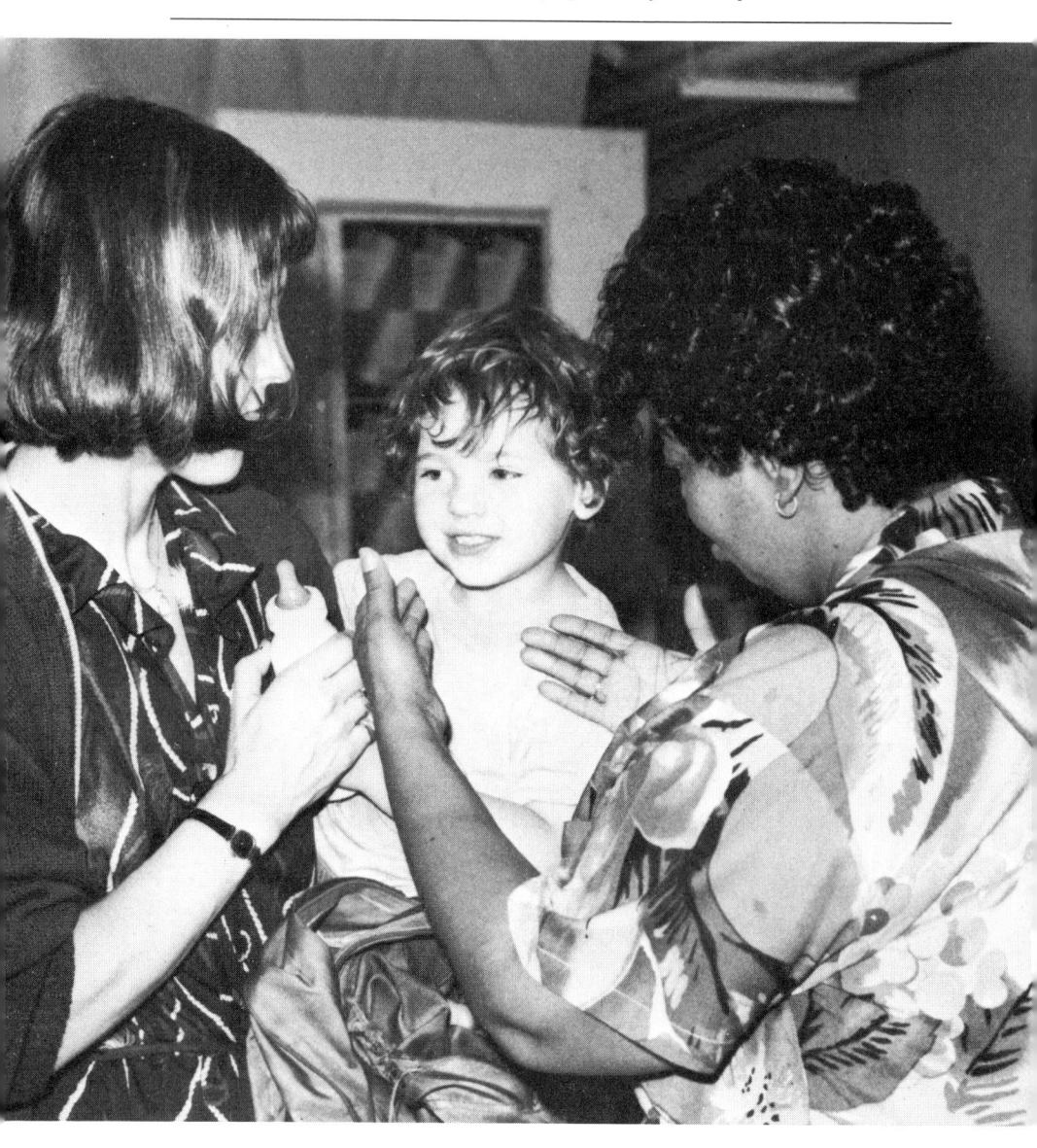

Chapter 5

Quality Indicators in Infant and Toddler Child Care: The Los Angeles Study

Carollee Howes

WHAT KIND OF CHILD CARE should we provide for infants and toddlers? The issues of whether or not young children should be in child care and, if they are to be in child care, what kind of care is optimal have loomed large in both professional and general public debates. The first half of the debate, whether infants and toddlers belong in child care at all, is no longer an issue. Recent statistics indicate that close to half of the mothers with infants 1 year old and younger are now in the paid labor force and all indications are that this percentage will only increase (O'Connell & Rogers, 1983).

The question of what type of care is best for children younger than 3 continues to be important. This chapter focuses on center-based care as it is the fastest growing form of care—for children of all ages (Hofferth & Phillips, 1987). In determining what is optimal center-based care I relied on three criteria: adult-child ratio, caregiver continuity, and caregiver training in child development. Each of these indicators has a conceptual relationship to the provision of good quality care and, as was discussed in Chapter 1, is associated with positive child and caregiver behaviors.

Adult-child ratio

The inclusion of the number of children cared for by each adult as a quality indicator rests on the assumption that much of the infant's or toddler's contact with the social and inanimate world is mediated by the adult caregiver. Through social games, verbal interaction, and physical contact, the caregiver provides a young child with a sense of security and enjoyment of social exchange. Moreover, the caregiver provides the infant or toddler with objects, highlights their properties, and engages with the

The number of children with whom each caregiver can engage in a stimulating and sensitive fashion is by necessity limited.

---

child in object play. Finally, by sensitive responses to the child's social signals the caregiver facilitates the child's development of a sense of self-worth. The number of children with whom each caregiver can engage in a stimulating and sensitive fashion is by necessity limited. With too many children to care for, the caregiver's interaction with each child becomes limited to feeding and diaper changing. Caregivers themselves report that a major cause of stress in their jobs is having too many children to care for and that in these cases their caregiving becomes routinized (Whitebook, Howes, Darrah, & Friedman, 1981).

One of the most important tasks of the infant-toddler period of development is establishing secure attachment relationships. Adaptive, secure attachments are fostered by caregivers who are warm and sensitive (Ainsworth, Blehar, Walters, & Wall, 1978). Such caregiving becomes difficult to provide with many children per caregiver.

Caregiver continuity

The infant's and toddler's sense of security in child care depends on the continuity or stability of caregivers. The child who forms an attachment relationship with an adult caregiver makes a smooth transition between home and child care and then uses the caregiver as a secure base during the day. Attachment formation is based in part on the availability and predictability of the caregiver. The child who experiences many different caregivers may not become attached to any of them and thus will fail to be secure in child care. The loss of an attachment figure can be very painful to a young child. The child who forms attachments to a series of caregivers, all of whom leave, may find it too painful to continue the cycle and conclude that human relationships are to be avoided.

Teacher training

Teacher training as a quality indicator of infant-toddler child care is probably the most controversial of the criteria selected for this study. Infant-toddler child care is relatively new. While child development training programs have trained preschool teachers for years, infant-toddler teacher training still lags behind present demand. Also, some people argue that infant-toddler teachers do not need to be trained, that experience as a mother is sufficient for the task.

The child who forms attachments to a series of caregivers may find it too painful to continue the cycle and conclude that human relationships are to be avoided.

Katz (1980) has pointed out that mothering and child care caregiving require different skills; for example, mothers' interaction with children is more emotional than teachers'. Caregivers trained in child development are more likely to plan care based on developmental expectations of appropriate behaviors; for example, a trained toddler teacher knows that exploring materials, such as in finger painting, is much more important than drill in letters and numbers. Training helps teachers justify and explain the choices of activities to parents. Trained caregivers are also better able to distinguish maladaptive behaviors from developmentally appropriate behaviors. These skills are particularly important as toddlers develop self-regulation. Finally, these caregivers are more likely to be aware of the issues involved in fostering secure attachment relationships in the children in their care.

Design of the research study

This research project was designed to compare child development and characteristics of families in eight child care centers judged to be high or low quality. The child outcomes studied in this reseach were development of self-regulation and compliance with adult requests; the family characteristics studied were stress and social support, patterns of interaction with the child, and satisfaction with child care.

Despite a decade of research on the effects of infant and toddler child care on child development, the literature on the effects of child care attendance on the development of self-regulation and compliance is contradictory. Specifically, Clarke-Stewart (1982) reports that children who attended child care were more socially mature than children who did not. However, Rubenstein, Howes, and Boyle (1981) report that child care children were less compliant and cooperative with adults than non-child care children.

One explanation for the discrepancy between studies may be the age of entry into child care. The children in Clarke-Stewart's study began child care as preschoolers whereas the children in the other study began as infants. Several theories of the development of self-regulation and compliance suggest that the toddler period is particularly important (Ainsworth, Blehar, Walters, & Wall, 1978; Kagan, 1981; Kopp, 1982). Perhaps the experience of some types of infant-toddler child care interferes with the development of self-control and compliance. Rubenstein et al. (1981) suggest that the differences found in child compliance may have been as

The pattern of behaviors of the teachers and parents of children in high quality child care suggests a consistently high degree of adult participation in the socialization of the child,

much a function of family interaction patterns as of child care experience.

One of the purposes of this project was to examine how variations in family characteristics were associated with child care attendance. We were particularly interested in differences in stress and social support. Families in which both parents work may experience chronic stress. The degree to which such stress interferes with competent parenting depends in part on the social support system of the family. We expected that high quality child care would serve as a social support and buffer some of the stress experienced by the family.

Eighty-nine families with children aged 18, 24, 30, and 36 months (all +/−3 weeks) participated in the study. The parents were middle class and well educated. Thirty-two families had a child enrolled in a high quality child care center, 25 had a child enrolled in a low quality center, and 32 families used no supplemental child care and were recruited through parent-child classes.

The centers were all community based and served full-tuition parents. The centers did not differ in tuition, in type of parent served, or in geographic locale. The research team spent a year in close contact with each center. This contact helped verify our placement of the center into the high or low category. High quality centers were defined as those centers with

- adult-child ratios of 1:4 or less in the 2-year-old and younger groups and 1:7 or less in the 30- and 36-month-old groups;
- turnover rates that resulted in children having only one or two primary teachers over a year; and
- teachers with formal training in child development.

From our year of observation we now believe that the high and low centers not only differed on the three criteria of quality — adult-child ratio, stability of caregivers, and training of caregivers — but also differed in philosophies concerning children and parents. In the high quality centers parents were involved in the day-to-day life of the center. They were welcome in classrooms, served on committees, and had some say in decision making. Parents were less involved in the low quality centers. However, these centers had perhaps a more realistic sense of the stressful nature of young working parents' lives. The low quality centers were open for longer hours; they served breakfast and dinner; and they did not expect parent participation.

Each family was seen four times. An initial 75-minute interview with the parents was used to collect information about family life. Home observations were made for an hour and a half during the time the family arrived

> *a persistence in resolving episodes, and a willingness on the part of adults to negotiate compromise.*

home for the evening and the child was put to bed. The child was also observed in child care during a transition period. Finally, the child and the primary parent participated in a 30-minute four-task laboratory session designed to measure compliance and self-control. A detailed description of all of these procedures and the associated measures can be found in Howes and Olenick (1986).

Differences in behavior of children from child care of varying quality

In the laboratory, children enrolled in child care were more likely than children at home to exhibit self-regulation (Howes & Olenick, 1986). Children enrolled in high quality child care centers were more likely to self-regulate than children in low quality child care centers. There were no differences between children with different child care experiences in their compliance with their parent.

At home all children and their parents negotiated compliance at an average rate of once every 3 minutes. There were no significant differences in children's behaviors associated with child care enrollment. In the child care centers, children enrolled in high quality programs were more compliant with the adults and less resistant to adult suggestions than children enrolled in low quality child care.

Differences in adult behaviors

Parents who enrolled their children in high quality child care were rated as more invested in or caring about their children's compliance both at home and in the laboratory than parents who enrolled their children in low quality child care (Howes & Olenick, 1986). At home, the parents who enrolled their children in low quality child care were more likely to use an angry tone to reprimand the child, while parents who used high quality child care or no child care were more likely to physically hold the child. Parents whose children were enrolled in high quality child care centers felt less helpless in their efforts to discipline their children than parents who used low quality care or were at home with their children (Golub, Howes, Goldenberg, Lee, & Olenick, 1984). Teachers in high quality child care centers were also rated as more invested and involved in compliance than teachers in low quality centers (Howes & Olenick, 1986).

Working parents who are more competent and confident in their parenting are more likely to be associated with high quality child care.

We also analyzed continuity between the behaviors used by the adults at home and in child care (Howes et al., 1984). The pattern of behaviors of the teachers and parents of children in high quality child care suggests a consistently high degree of adult participation in the socialization of the child, a persistence in resolving episodes, and a willingness on the part of adults to negotiate compromise. In contrast, the pattern of behaviors of the teachers and parents in the low quality centers suggests both a lack of attentiveness to the child and an expectation of unidirectionality of the socialization process in that adults are to give directions and children are to obey. Thus, the child in each environment received a relatively consistent pattern of socialization.

Differences in family characteristics

As we expected, parents who enrolled their children in child care reported more complex and stressful lives than parents in families in which only one parent worked (Howes & Olenick, 1986). Parents who enrolled their children in low quality child care reported more stress than parents who enrolled their children in high quality child care. There were no differences between family groups in reported integration into social support networks. However, parents who enrolled their children in high quality child care were more satisfied with their child care than parents who enrolled their child in low quality child care (Howes & Olenick, 1983). Thus, child care may serve as a source of social support for the parents with children in high quality child care. In contrast, child care quality appears to be a source of additional stress for parents of children enrolled in low quality child care.

Discussion and conclusions

The results of this study suggest that children and their families can benefit from high quality center child care for infants and toddlers. The community-based centers that had good adult-child ratios and stable, trained caregivers provided care that enhanced the development of the children and supported the families that used the care. The situation is, of course, more complex than this. Our study suggests that not only do good things within child care go together, but that working parents who have

Both families and children appear to have more optimal development when infant and toddler child care includes one adult for a small number of children, stable caregivers, and caregiver training.

---

less stressful lives and are more competent and confident in their parenting are more likely to be associated with high quality child care. In fact, family and child care characteristics combined better explained the child's behavior in the laboratory than the quality of child care alone (Howes & Olenick, 1986).

There are a number of explanations for the association between family and child care characteristics. Child care for infants and toddlers is very hard to find. All of the centers, but particularly the high quality centers, had long waiting lists. In fact, not all families who put their names on the waiting lists months before the children were born were able to get spaces in the centers. Putting an unborn child on a child care waiting list implies a commitment to both working and planning for the well-being of the child and family. Families under stress are less able to make this kind of advanced commitment or to do the time-consuming research necessary —to ask questions, make informed decisions, and visit many different child care facilities. Stressed families may also feel that they need the longer hours of the low quality centers or that the expected participation in the high quality centers exceeds their available time.

We observed the families and centers for a relatively brief period. Perhaps families who enrolled their children in the low quality centers might have appeared less stressed and more like the families with children in high quality care if they too had used high quality care. If this hypothesis has some merit, then the effect of trained teachers in child care may go beyond the effect on the child. Steinberg and Green (1979) report that mothers who use center care feel that their relationship with their child was improved as a function of contact with the center. The consistency between teacher and parent behaviors suggests that the parents may have been observing teachers for suggestions of ways to engage with their child. The teachers and parents in the high quality centers appeared to be, according to experts in the field, more competent in child socialization and parenting. Thus, the trained teachers may also have been engaged in informal parent education.

This chapter opened with the question, "What kind of child care should we provide for infants and toddlers?" The results of this study suggest expanding the question to read, "What kind of child care should we be providing for children and families?" Both families and children appear to come closer to optimal development when infant and toddler child care includes one adult for a small number of children, stable caregivers, and caregiver training.

References

Ainsworth, M., Blehar, M., Walters, E., & Wall, S. (1978). *Patterns of attachment.* Hillsdale, NJ: Erlbaum.

Clarke-Stewart, A. (1982). *Daycare.* Cambridge, MA: Harvard University Press.

Golub, J., Howes, C., Goldenberg, C., Lee, M., & Olenick, M. (1984). *A comparison of discipline techniques of daycare and non-daycare parents.* Paper presented at the Annual American Educational Research Association Meeting, New Orleans.

Hofferth, S., & Phillips, D. (1987). Maternal labor force participation and child care: 1970–1995. *Journal of Marriage and the Family, 49,* 559–571.

Howes, C., Goldenberg, C., Golub, J., Lee, M., & Olenick, M. (1984). *Continuity in socialization experiences in home and day care.* Paper presented at the Annual American Educational Research Association Meeting, New Orleans.

Howes, C., & Olenick, M. (1983). *Parent selection of high and low quality day care.* Workshop presented at the National Association for Young Children Annual Conference, Atlanta.

Howes, C., & Olenick, M. (1986). Family and child care influences on toddler compliance. *Child Development, 57,* 202–216.

Kagan, J. (1981). *The second year.* Cambridge, MA: Harvard University Press.

Katz, L. (1980). Mothering and teaching: Some significant distinctions. In L. Katz (Ed.), *Current topics in early childhood education* (Vol. 3) (pp. 47–63). Norwood, NJ: Ablex.

Kopp, C. (1982). The antecedents of self regulation. *Developmental Psychology, 18,* 199–214.

O'Connell, M., & Rogers, C. (1983). *Child care arrangements for working mothers: June, 1982* (Current population reports, Series P-23, No. 129). Washington, DC: U.S. Government Printing Office.

Rubenstein, J., Howes, C., & Boyle, P. (1981). A two year follow-up of infants in community based daycare. *Journal of Child Psychology and Psychiatry, 22,* 209–218.

Steinberg, L., & Green, C. (1979). *How parents may mediate the effects of daycare.* Paper presented at the Biennial Meeting of the Society for Research in Child Development, San Francisco.

Whitebook, M., Howes, C., Darrah, R., & Friedman, J. (1981). Who's minding the child care worker? *Children Today, 10,* 2–6.

Chapter 6

Effects of Child Care, Family, and Individual Characteristics on Children's Language Development: The Victoria Day Care Research Project

Hillel Goelman and Alan R. Pence

IN THIS CHAPTER we report data drawn from a 2-year study of children, parents, and caregivers in licensed center care, licensed family day care, and unlicensed family day care. The chapter discusses the question of quality from several perspectives: characteristics of the child care provider, child care environment, and program; children's experiences in child care; and children's performance on standardized measures of language development and within the context of family background.

Our study was based on examination of structure and process variables in both child care and home environments. This perspective is supported by a number of studies that have documented the influence of family structure variables (i.e., maternal marital status, level of education, employment situation, income) and family process variables (mother-child interactions, parental stress factors, attitudes toward child care) on children's behavior and performance on developmental outcome measures (Bee et al., 1982; Hetherington, Cox, & Cox, 1979; Stuckey, McGhee, & Bell, 1982; Thompson, Lamb, & Estes, 1982).

In order to examine some of the relationships between family structure variables, child care setting, and children's performance on measures of expressive and receptive language development, Goelman and Pence (1987) compared children from high- and low-*resource* families. The data strongly suggested that children from low-resource families — that is, families headed by single mothers with low levels of education, occupation, and income — tended to be disproportionately enrolled in low quality family day care settings. Maternal marital status, occupation, and education level contributed significantly to the children's scores on the Peabody Picture Vocabulary Test (PPVT) (Dunn, 1979) and the Expressive One-Word Picture Vocabulary Test (EOWPVT) (Gardner, 1979). The finding that children from low-resource families were overrepresented in lower quality family day care homes with less educated caregivers drew attention to the fact that the level of caregiver education was also a significant predictor of children's scores on these measures.

Family structure variables, therefore, appeared to be associated with both the children's performance on the measures of language development and the selection of child care settings. In this chapter we continue to examine these patterns by studying the relationship between indexes of child care quality, in terms of both the social structure of the child care environment and the children's daily experiences in this setting, and the children's performance on the two language measures used in this study.

Method

The Victoria Day Care Research Project was conducted from 1983 to 1985 with children, parents, and caregivers in licensed child care centers, licensed family day care homes, and unlicensed family day care homes. The study took place in Victoria, the capital of British Columbia, which has a metropolitan area population of approximately 250,000. (Please consult Goelman & Pence, 1985, 1987; or Pence, Charlesworth, & Goelman, 1986 for detailed information on the design, methodology, and subject pool in this study.) A total of 105 child-parent-caregiver triads participated in this study. The children were in care for approximately 30 hours per week while their mothers were working, looking for work, or studying. The study included approximately equal numbers of boys and girls who were either first born or only children and were drawn from approximately equal numbers of one- and two-parent families. (See Table 6-1 for a breakdown of the subject pool.) No significant differences existed between the groups on such characteristics as levels of parental education, occupation, and income; and ages at which the children entered child care (see Table 6-2). As in Clarke-Stewart's work (1981, 1986), the mean age of children in center care (50.5 months) was higher than the mean age of children in licensed family day care (38.8) and unlicensed family day care (39.8), largely due to the fact that most child care centers in Victoria did not enroll children younger than age 3.

There were three major components of the study: outcome measures, observations, and interviews (see Figure 6-1). The PPVT and EOWPVT

Table 6-1. Numbers of Parent, Child, and Caregiver Participants in the Victoria Day Care Research Project

	Parents and children					
	One-parent		Two-parent			
	Boys	Girls	Boys	Girls	Total	Caregivers
Center child care	14	13	15	11	53	25
Licensed family day care	4	7	7	9	27	24
Unlicensed family day care	7	7	6	5	25	25
Total	25	27	28	25	105	74

Table 6-2. Background Information on Subject Pool in the Victoria Day Care Research Project

	Licensed family day care		Unlicensed family day care		Center child care	
	Mean	SD	Mean	SD	Mean	SD
Age of child	38.81	10.16	39.78	11.41	50.56	4.37[a]
Age began care[b]	17.94	11.20	16.46	11.68	19.30	12.58
Total time in care[b]	20.86	12.25	23.81	11.98	31.26	14.24[a]
Time in current care[b]	12.28	11.35	13.81	11.80	13.18	4.95
Hours mother works/week	34.33	6.79	33.38	7.19	36.34	8.56
Mother's age (years)	28.52	5.57	28.51	3.52	30.32	4.20
Mother's educational level[c]	3.50	1.28	3.65	1.42	3.96	1.34
Mother's income level[d]	3.05	1.25	3.22	1.40	3.30	1.60
Mother's job level[e]	3.28	1.07	3.20	1.54	3.34	1.10
Partner's educational level[c]	3.55	1.39	3.38	1.32	4.75	1.45[a]
Partner's income level[d]	5.10	1.62	4.42	1.55	5.09	1.78
Partner's job level[e]	3.09	1.60	3.33	1.34	3.29	1.51

[a] CDC > LFDC, UFDC $p < .001$ (one way ANOVA)
[b] All child-related variables are in months.
[c] Education level scale: 1 = grade school, 2 = some high school, 3 = high school graduate, 4 = some junior college or technical school, 5 = junior college graduate, 6 = university graduate.
[d] Income level scale: 1 = less than $5,000, 2 = $5,000–$8,999, 3 = $9,000–$14,999, 4 = $15,000–$19,999, 5 = $20,000–$24,999, 6 = $25,000–$29,999, 7 = $30,000 and more.
[e] Based on modified Blishen scale.

were administered to the children on three different occasions at 6-month intervals. The parents and caregivers participated in structured 1-hour interviews covering a wide range of topics including family background, employment history, education, child care needs, and attitudes toward current child care arrangements. The results of the interviews are found in Pence and Goelman (1986, 1987, in press).

The observations were conducted using two types of instruments. To assess quality aspects of the structure of the child care setting, we used parallel rating forms designed for center and family day care environments: the Early Childhood Environment Rating Scale (ECERS) (Harms & Clifford, 1980) and the Day Care Home Environment Rating Scale (DCHERS) (Harms, Clifford, & Padan-Belkin, 1983). These scales consist

Figure 6-1. Research Components in the Victoria Day Care Project

Outcome measures
  Peabody Picture Vocabulary Test
  Expressive One-Word Picture Vocabulary Test
  Preschool Interpersonal Problem Solving Test (PIPS)
  Child questionnaire

Observation components
  The Early Childhood Environment Rating Scale
  Child Observation Form
  Caregiver Post-Impression Form
  Child Post-Impression Form

Parent questionnaire
  Child care history and research
  Present child care arrangement and focal child
  Parent's perception of the caregiver
  Opinions on working mothers
  Parent's satisfaction with arrangement
  Child management situations
  Personal job history

Caregiver questionnaire
  Caregiver's history
  Supply of and/or search for children
  Caregiver's perception of the parent and child
  Caregiver's perception of the child care environment and the child
  Caregiver's satisfaction with the child care arrangement
  Child management situations
  Caregiver's family background, work history, and health

of more than 30 discrete items clustered in a number of subscales and yield a total rating score as well. The items are rated on a 1 to 7 point scale and cover such areas as space and furnishings, learning materials, and social development.

The Child Observation Form (COF) (Goelman, 1983), a time and event sampling instrument, was used to observe child care centers (Ruopp, Travers, Glantz, & Coelen, 1979) and family day care homes (Stallings & Porter, 1980). The form allowed observers to record children's play partners and the types of activities in which they were engaged. Observers who had passed a training program and achieved an 85% level of interrater reliability observed children for 5-second windows. The focal children were observed on 2 different days within a 10-day period for a total of 6 hours of observation. The COF was used for 1 hour during morning free play periods on both observation days. These observations generated more than 240 windows of spontaneous play of children in their child care setting. The respective rating scales (ECERS and DCHERS) were completed at the conclusion of the 6 hours of observation.

Results

In this section data will be presented on the characteristics of the child care providers, the structure of the child care settings, and the children's family backgrounds; the nature of the children's experiences in child care; and the relationship of these variables to the children's performance on the standardized measures of language development.

From the information gathered during the caregiver interview (see Pence & Goelman, in press, for a detailed report on these data), a number of distinctive characteristics of the three groups of caregivers emerged. Differences cited regarding these data were all significant to the .05 level using z tests for independent proportions. While 100% of the center child care workers reported having formal training in early childhood education (a legal prerequisite), significantly fewer licensed (29.2%) and unlicensed (22.2%) family day care caregivers had formal training. Conversely, significantly more licensed (95.8%) and unlicensed (92.6%) family day care caregivers reported experience as a parent than the center workers (52%). Further, significantly more licensed (95.8%) and unlicensed (92.6%) family day care caregivers reported experience as "caregivers to other children" than the center workers (60%).

When asked questions regarding their work and future career plans, the groups of child care providers continued to show pronounced differences.

Both center and licensed family day care providers reported levels of job satisfaction significantly higher than their unlicensed family day care counterparts.

Both center and licensed family day care providers reported levels of job satisfaction significantly higher than their unlicensed family day care counterparts. A significantly higher proportion of unlicensed (51.9%) than licensed (16.6%) family day care providers reported that they would prefer other employment. In terms of their reasons for providing care, significantly more licensed (92.3%) than unlicensed (72.7%) family day care providers indicated that they enjoyed being with children. Conversely, significantly more unlicensed (36.4%) than licensed (10.3%) family day care providers said they were in child care because it provided a playmate for their own children. When the unlicensed family day care providers were asked about the type of work they would prefer to be doing, only 7.4% indicated child care; 14.8% cited "child-oriented" work; while 29.6% reported a preference for "non-child-oriented" work.

What was the quality of the 25 centers, 24 licensed family day care homes and 25 unlicensed family day cay care homes who participated in this study? A preliminary answer to this question is found in the subscale and total scores generated by the ECERS and DCHERS. These scores were seen as indexes of aspects of the structure of the child care settings by rating such characteristics as the quantity, quality, availability, and accessibility of various materials and furnishings.

Although the ECERS and the DCHERS were similar in construction, their differences in specific items and scoring criteria prohibited direct statistical comparisons between the center and family day care environments (see Table 6-3). Nonetheless, the mean scores do provide a general context for the consideration of the quality of these settings. The unlicensed family day care settings, for example, scored as high as 3 (i.e., minimal) on only one subscale and had consistently lower scores than the licensed family day care and center settings on every subscale as well as for the total. Similarly, the licensed family day care settings consistently scored lower than the center settings.

In order to address the question of quality in terms of the children's experiences in care, analyses of variance were performed on the children's activities as recorded on the Child Observation Forms (COF). As shown in Table 6-4, the children in unlicensed family day care engaged in solitary play significantly more than children in center programs. The children in both types of family day care engaged in parallel play significantly more than the children in centers. The children in centers were observed in cooperative play significantly more than children in family day care settings.

Table 6-3. Subscale and Total Scores for ECERS and DCHERS in 3 Types of Child Care*

	Licensed family day care	Unlicensed family day care	Center child care
Space and furnishings	3.55	2.97	4.8
Basic care	3.24	2.78	4.8
Language	3.36	2.78	4.4
Learning	3.57	3.06	4.8
Social development	3.02	2.40	4.31
Adult needs	4.03	2.42	4.0
Total	3.35	2.82	4.62

* 1 = Poor, 3 = Minimal, 5 = Good, 7 = Excellent.

Table 6-4. Number of Episodes of Types of Play in Child Observations in Licensed Family Day Care, Unlicensed Family Day Care, and Center Child Care

	Licensed family day care	Unlicensed family day care	Center child care	F	$p<$
Solitary	6.82	10.63	6.64	3.79	.025
Parallel	51.03	47.34	37.71	7.02	.001
Cooperative	42.14	42.02	55.63	8.83	.001
Pair	35.75	28.55	16.55	9.22	.001
Group	49.63	43.79	72.15	15.97	.001

There were great similarities across the three types of care in some of the children's play activities and striking differences in others. For example, no significant differences were found in the total number of play episodes observed on reading (avg. 8.2%), gross motor (avg. 10.1%), structured fine motor (avg. 10.3%), art and music (avg. 16.6%), conversation (avg. 19.9%), and dramatic play (avg. 21%).

The two major differences that emerged were in the use of television and the frequency of interactions coded as *information*. Children in unlicensed family day care were observed viewing educational television more frequently (7.6% of the time) than children in either licensed family day care (3.7%) or center programs (.01%) ($F = 11.65$, $p < .001$). Further, children in unlicensed family day care were observed watching noneducational television more frequently (2.7%) than children in licensed family

The unlicensed family day care settings were consistently lower than the licensed family day care and center settings on every subscale as well as the total score.

day care (1.3%) and center programs (where it was never observed). These data confirm the caregivers' reports of the frequency of television watching. When asked whether the focal child ever watched television while in care, significantly fewer center workers (16.7%) answered affirmatively than did the licensed (76.9%) and unlicensed (79.9%) family day care providers.

Information activities are those interactions, not necessarily in the context of formal instruction, where specific informational content is conveyed from the caregiver to the children. This interaction was originally so labeled by Wells (1975) in a taxonomy of adult-child discourse functions. McCartney (1984) included the category in her analyses of adult-child interactions in child care centers and found this interaction to be a significant and positive predictor of children's scores on the PPVT. In this study, children in center programs were observed in *informational* exchanges significantly more frequently (9.4%) than children in either unlicensed (5.1%) or licensed (3.4%) family day care ($F=7.89$, $p < .001$). These results, together with McCartney's, are examined in greater detail in the final section of this chapter.

We conducted correlational analyses on the ECERS and the DCHERS and the children's activities as recorded on the COF. The only activity segment that correlated with either rating scale was *information*. This activity correlated positively and significantly ($p < .05$) with the DCHERS subscales on learning (.36), social development (.41), language development (.46), and total score (.44) and with the ECERS subscales on language (.33), learning (.35), social development (.28), and total score (.27).

To this point the analyses focused primarily on examining the quality of the child care settings in terms of their structure and process characteristics and on considering the relationships between the characteristics. The next step was to examine the relationships between these indexes and the children's performances on developmental outcome measures.

The children's PPVT and EOWPVT scores correlated with aspects of the family day care settings but not with those in the center environments. The PPVT correlated significantly ($p < .05$) with the DCHERS subscale on social development (.51) and the total rating score (.33). The EOWPVT correlated with the total score (.32) and the subscales on learning materials (.33) and social development (.48). These findings were extended by subsequent regression analyses that demonstrated that, while the DCHERS total rating scores predicted approximately 14% of the variance on the PPVT ($p < .05$) and 13% of the variance on the EOWPVT ($p < .01$), the ECERS scores did not. No correlations were found between the frequency of the children's play activities in either the center or family day care settings and the children's performance on the outcome measures.

A series of 3 (type of care) × 2 (one-parent/two-parent families) analyses on the EOWPVT revealed significant differences ($F = 3.11$, $p < .04$) between the scores of the children in unlicensed (98.6) and licensed (109.3) family day care and center programs (107.3). No significant differences were found in the mean scores of children from the two types of family structure. The results on the PPVT were consistent with those on the EOWPVT. The differences between the mean scores of the children in unlicensed family day care (93.4) and both licensed family day care (101.1) and center day care (101.2) resulted in a main effect approaching significance ($F = 2.29$, $p < .10$). The differences between the scores of children in two-parent families (102.1) and one-parent families (96.3) also approached significance ($F = 3.54$, $p < .06$).

Taken together, the data presented to this point suggest possible relationships between aspects of child care structure and process, child care structure and developmental outcomes, and family structure and developmental outcomes. Using the quantitative inferential, correlational, and regression analyses as reference points, we conducted subsequent data analyses to achieve a more qualitative examination of the relationships between child care structure, child care process, and children's performance on the two measures of language development.

Computer searches were conducted to identify those centers and family day care homes that, on the basis of their respective ECERS and DCHERS scores, were either one standard deviation above (high quality) or below (low quality) the mean scores for the settings in this study. After these had been identified, a wide range of data (including mean test scores and information on the daily activities of the children) was generated on the high and low quality center and family day care settings. Since assumptions of randomness could not be made due to the manner in which the high and low quality settings were selected, inferential tests and comparisons between the groups are not appropriate. The differences cited here, therefore, are treated as descriptive and illustrative only. As noted, however, this information both confirms the results yielded by the quantitative analyses previously cited and lends further depth and clarity to those findings.

As indicated in Table 6-5, there were few differences between the high and low quality center environments. While their mean ECERS scores did differ (206 vs. 143), the high ($n = 14$) and low ($n = 12$) quality center environments were quite similar on such items as mean scores on

Children in unlicensed family day care watched television more frequently than children in the other two types of programs.

Table 6-5. Characteristics of High and Low Quality Family Day Care and Center Child Care Environments

	High family day care	Low family day care	High center child care	Low center child care
Mean PPVT scores	98.42	83.30	99.21	104.21
Mean EOWPVT scores	109.03	86.63	107.00	107.25
Quality	134.93	69.63	206.00	143.25
Structured fine motor	10.34	6.60	7.27	14.03
Art, music	18.71	11.41	12.96	19.01
Dramatic play	14.53	28.70	19.14	26.74
Gross motor	16.84	6.43	13.65	9.03
Information	6.30	1.48	10.69	5.97
Reading	7.68	4.82	6.06	13.06
Educational TV	3.03	12.39	.00	.07
Non educational TV	.99	5.37	.00	.00

language development tests and style and type of play activity. This pattern suggests that, despite rating differences, the center environments were quite homogeneous and shared a rather narrow range of quality and variation. This would certainly be consistent with the absence of correlation and predictive power in the ECERS reported above.

In sharp contrast, the high and low quality family day care settings revealed distinct and largely predictable differences. (Of the 15 high quality homes, 13 were licensed; of the 11 low quality homes, only two were licensed.) Mean test scores on both the PPVT and EOWPVT were 15 to 23 points higher in the high quality home settings. Children in the high quality family day care programs engaged in more structured fine motor, art and music, gross motor, information, and reading activities than children in the low quality family day care programs. The categories for which higher frequencies were observed in the low quality family day care settings were participating in dramatic play and watching educational and noneducational television.

These results suggest that both type and quality of care interact with children's performance on standardized measures of language development. The following discussion considers these findings in the context of the previously reported results on the impact of family background variables on the children and in light of related studies that have examined these questions from similar theoretical and methodological perspectives.

Level of caregiver education was a significant predictor of the children's test performance.

Discussion

The results reported here replicate, complement, and extend those reported in other multimethodological studies of the impact of child care and family background variables on young children. No one single variable (i.e., type of care, structure, daily experiences, family background) sufficiently explained children's performance on measures of receptive and expressive language development. Rather, the data strongly suggested a complex interaction of child care structure and process variables within the contexts of family resources and the factors involved in the selection of child care settings by individual families.

Differences emerged among the three types of care in both structure and process variables. Centers were generally rated higher than both types of family day care homes for the total score and subscale scores on the rating scales of child care quality. Play and activity patterns differed: Higher frequencies of developmentally facilitative interactions were found in the two licensed forms of day care (informational) and higher frequencies of less facilitative experiences (solitary play, television watching) in the unlicensed family day care homes.

Quality of care in the family day care settings appeared to be much more variable, and a much more potent predictor of children's language development, than quality in the centers. Structural indexes of family day care quality were associated with the children's performances on measures of receptive and expressive language development. Level of caregiver education (higher in the licensed group) was also found to be a significant predictor of the children's performance on the tests used. Striking differences were found between the highest and lowest quality family day care homes along a number of dimensions, including mean test scores and children's involvement in developmentally facilitative activities.

These findings are largely consistent with those revealed in the Bermuda Study. Similar to results reported in McCartney's analyses of home and child care center influences on children's language development (McCartney, 1984; McCartney, Scarr, Phillips, Grajek, & Schwarz, 1982; Phillips, Scarr, & McCartney, this volume), our study found that
- maternal education level was a significant predictor of children's performance on the PPVT,
- the frequency of informational utterances by the child care teachers positively correlated with the overall quality of the settings, and

Children in unlicensed family day care were observed in solitary play significantly more frequently than children in licensed family day care and center settings.

- significant correlations existed between most of the subscale and total quality ratings on the ECERS.

While McCartney reported a direct relationship between the ECERS and PPVT scores, we did not find this for the centers in the Victoria Day Care Research Project. However, we did find this relationship between the rating scale scores and both the PPVT and EOWPVT scores for the family day care homes.

Like the Chicago Study (Clarke-Stewart, 1986; this volume), our study also found differences between the quality of child care structure in centers and in family day care homes. Similarly, both studies reported higher frequencies of informational teaching or verbal exchanges in the centers than in the family day care homes. Higher frequencies of TV watching were reported in the family day care homes than in the centers in both studies. While Clarke-Stewart found no differences on levels of cognitive development between the children in center and family day care, we found those differences in this study. This is more than likely due to the inclusion of children from a wider range of family backgrounds in a wider range of family day care settings in the Victoria study than in the Clarke-Stewart sample, which was drawn from a largely middle- to upper-class population consisting of all two-parent families.

Despite these differences in subject pool, other similarities between the results of the two studies stand out. For example, both studies report high correlations between quality of child care structure, level of caregiver education, and children's performance on measures of cognitive development. Clarke-Stewart's finding of positive correlations between test performance and caregiver-child reading episodes and negative correlations between test performance and frequencies of solitary play are also paralleled in the Victoria data. Children in higher quality family day care settings, with higher mean test scores, participated in more reading episodes than children in lower quality family day care settings. Further, the children who received the lowest mean test scores were those in unlicensed family day care settings, which received uniformly low quality ratings. Additionally, these children were observed in solitary play significantly more frequently than children in licensed family day care and center settings.

The inclusion of both center and family day care settings; a range of both good and poor environments within both types of care; and the use of observation, tests, and interviews have enhanced the generalizability of studies that have identified important structure and process variables within child care settings. Including children from a range of family

More developmentally facilitative play was found in licensed family day care and center programs.

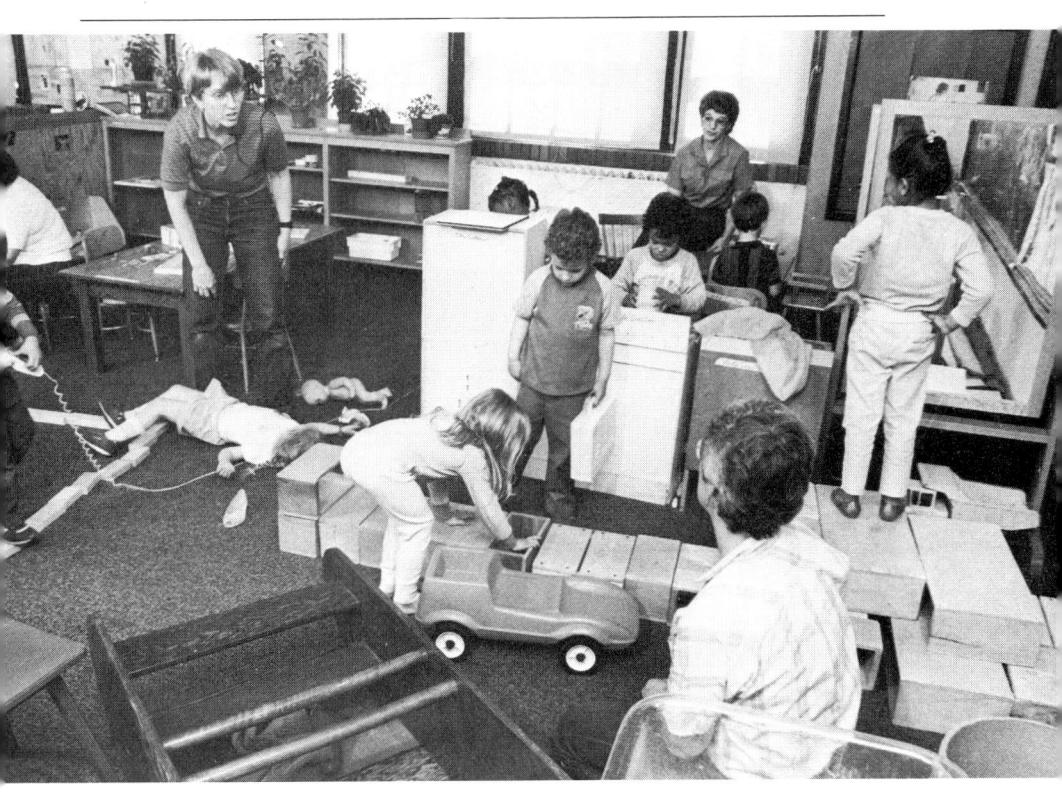

backgrounds has yielded valuable information on some of the broader contextual factors within which the child care experiences are embedded.

It is of note and concern that a significant number of children in these studies appeared to have a "worst of both worlds" situation: They come from low-resource families and attend low quality family day care. This pattern suggests a kind of mirror image of the data reported by Carew's (1980) study of home and child care influences on children's development. Carew found that developmentally facilitative experiences in home and child care settings for middle-class children contribute to the children's successful performance on developmental outcome measures. In our study, it appears that the flip side of the coin may also be true in a more ominous sense. Children from homes characterized by lower levels of economic and educational resources attend family day care homes run by women with lower levels of training, interest, and commitment. These

Children who come from low resource families generally attend low quality family day care.

---

settings are generally rated as being of minimal quality in terms of the physical environment and the kinds of materials available to the children. The interactions, experiences, and activities the children had while in care were not considered to provide the optimal conditions for child development.

The data reported here strongly suggest that aspects of family structure, child care structure, and child care process have a strong effect upon the development of the young child. To further flesh out the ecological complexity of the family day care interface, this tripod of information needs to be bolstered by information regarding the nature of developmentally facilitative processes, interactions, and experiences within the child's home setting. Specifically, information on adult-child language interactions in a range of family backgrounds (i.e., Cross, Parmenter, Juchnowski, & Johnson, 1984; Tizard & Hughes, 1984) would greatly enhance the clarity of the findings revealed in this study. This information, from one of the major microsystems within which the child participates, is necessary but not sufficient to gain an understanding of the complex interaction of factors within and across the systemic levels of the ecology of child care.

The results of this study strongly suggest that further inquiry into the definition and effects of various levels of child care quality must consider not just the relationships between measurable characteristics of environments, activities, and outcomes, but also at least some of the broader socioeconomic factors that affect the delivery and availability of alternatives from which parents select their child care arrangements. Toward this end, research on the effects of child care must continue to focus on both the discrete pieces of the puzzle and the complex ways in which those pieces fit together.

References

Bee, H.L., Barnard, K.E., Eyres, S.J., Gray, L.A., Hammond, M.A., Apietz, A.L., Snyder, C., & Clark, B. (1982). Prediction of IQ and language skill from perinatal status, child performance, family characteristics, and mother-infant interaction. *Child Development, 53,* 1134–1156.

Carew, J.V. (1980). Experience and development of intelligence in young children at home and in day care. *Monographs of the Society for Research in Child Development, 45*(6–7, Serial No. 187).

Clarke-Stewart, K.A. (1981). Observation and experiment: Complementary strategies for studying day care and social development. In S. Kilmer (Ed.), *Advances in Early Education and Day Care* (Vol. 2) (pp. 227–250). Greenwich, CT: JAI Press.

Clarke-Stewart, K.A. (1986). Family day care: A home away from home? *Children's Environment Quarterly, 3*(1).
Cross, T., Parmenter, G., Juchnowski, M., & Johnson, G. (1984). Effects of day care experience on the formal and pragmatic development of young children. In C.L. Thew & C.E. Johnson (Eds.), *Proceedings of the Second International Congress for the Study of Child Language, Volume II*. New York: University Press of America.
Dunn, L.M. (1979). *Peabody Picture Vocabulary Test—Revised*. American Guidance Service, Publishers' Bldg., Circle Pines, MN 55014.
Gardner M.F. (1979). *Expressive One-Word Picture Vocabulary Test*. Novato, CA: Academic Therapy Publications.
Goelman, H. (1983). Manual for observing in day care centers and homes. Unpublished manuscript, University of British Columbia, Vancouver.
Goelman, H., & Pence, A.R. (1985). The ecology of day care in Canada: A research agenda for the 1980's. *Canadian Journal of Education, 10*(4), 323–344.
Goelman, H., & Pence, A.R. (1987). Some aspects of the relationships between family structure and child language development in three types of day care. In D.L. Peters & S. Kontos (Eds.), *Annual Advances in Applied Developmental Psychology, Volume II: Continuity and Discontinuity of Experience in Child Care* (pp. 129–146). Norwood, NJ: Ablex.
Harms, T., & Clifford, R. (1980). *The Early Childhood Environment Rating Scale*. New York: Teachers College Press, Columbia University.
Harms, T., Clifford, R., & Padan-Belkin, E. (1983). *The Day Care Home Environment Rating Scale*. Homebased Day Care Training Project, Frank Porter Graham Child Development Center, 500 NCNB Plaza, Chapel Hill, NC 27514.
Hetherington, E.M., Cox, M., & Cox, R. (1979). Play and social interaction in children following divorce. *Journal of Social Issues, 35*(4), 26–49.
McCartney, K. (1984). Effects of quality of day care environment on children's language development. *Developmental Psychology, 20*(2), 244–260.
McCartney, K., Scarr, S., Phillips, D., Grajek, S., & Schwarz, J.C. (1982). Environmental differences among day care centers and their effects on children's development. In E. Zigler & E. Gordon (Eds.), *Day care: Science and social policy issues*. Boston: Auburn House.
Pence, A.R., Charlesworth, M., & Goelman, H. (1986). Applying Bronfenbrenner's ecological model to a study of daycare in a Canadian city. *The Canadian Journal of Child Care, 10*(1 & 2), 107–114.
Pence, A.R., & Goelman, H. (1986). The Victoria Day Care Research Project: Initial descriptive data on parents. *Canadian Children, 10*(1 & 2), 115–124.
Pence, A.R., & Goelman, H. (1987). Silent partners: Parents of children in three types of day care. *Early Childhood Research Quarterly, 2*(2), 103–118.
Pence, A.R., & Goelman, H. (in press). Who cares for the child in day care? An examination of caregivers from three types of care. *Early Childhood Research Quarterly*.
Ruopp, R.R., Travers, J., Glantz, F., & Coelen, C. (1979). *Children at the center: Final report of the National Day Care Study*. Cambridge, MA: Abt Associates.
Stallings, J., & Porter, A. (1980). *Observation component of the National Day Care Home Study: Volume 3*. Washington, DC: U.S. Department of Health and Human Services.

Stuckey, M.F., McGhee, P.E., & Bell, N.J. (1982). Parent-child interaction: The influence of maternal employment. *Developmental Psychology, 18*(4), 635–644.

Thompson, R.A., Lamb, M.E., & Estes, D. (1982). Stability of infant-mother attachment and its relationship to changing life circumstances in an unselected middle-class sample. *Child Development, 53,* 144–148.

Tizard, B., & Hughes, M. (1984). *Young children learning: Talking and thinking at home and at school.* London: Fontana.

Wells, G. (1975). The context of children's language experiences. *Educational Review, 27,* 114–125.

Material in this chapter was presented originally at the Annual Conference of the American Educational Research Association, San Francisco, April, 1986. The research reported here was supported by the Social Sciences and Humanities Research Council of Canada. The authors thank Maxine Charlesworth, Lorraine Toleikis, and Warren Weir for their assistance in data collection and analysis.

Chapter 7

In Search of Consistencies in Child Care Research

K. Alison Clarke-Stewart

RECENT CHILD CARE research has been in waves. The first wave, in the early 1970s, was when researchers asked "Is child care good or bad?" In the second wave, in the late 1970s, they asked "What are the effects of different kinds of child care?" Now, it seems, we are in the midst of a third wave of research. Researchers are asking more complex questions such as "How do child care qualities combine with family factors to produce effects on children's development?"

The metaphor of child care research waves is apt, in more than the obvious way. For in each wave, it seems, researchers become engulfed by measures, methods, and mixed results, and often are in danger of drowning in data. So it is in this monograph: There are five different studies representative of this newest wave of research. They present five quite different stories. I suspect that we could add more different stories if more researchers had contributed chapters on their child care research. For now, though, it is enough just to confine our discussion to the studies we have here. They are on the crest of the new wave of child care research, and if there is anything robust and significant in the research, it should show up in this sample of five.

What then, can we make out of these five different studies and their five different stories — other than a monograph? Can we find consistencies? Can we explain discrepancies? Do we know more now than when we started about the predictors of quality child care? It is difficult enough to interpret the results of any *one* of these studies. Can we integrate and make sense of all five?

To begin, let me recap the basic statistics of the five studies: In the

Chicago Study, we surveyed eighty 2- to 5-year-olds from intact, primarily middle-class families, who were in one of the following arrangements: at home with a caregiver, in a family day care home, in a center part-time, or in a center full-time. More than 60 child care facilities were included. Deborah Phillips, Sandra Scarr, and Kathleen McCartney studied 166 children from 3 to 5 years old in nine child care centers in Bermuda. A third team, Susan Kontos and Richard Fiene, studied one hundred 3- to 5-year-olds, from 10 centers representative of child care in northeastern Pennsylvania. In Los Angeles, Carollee Howes observed 89 middle-class children, 1½ to 3 years old, who were in four high quality centers, four low quality centers, or no child care at all. In a fifth study, Hillel Goelman and Alan Pence studied 105 first-born 2- to 5-year-olds, from one- or two-parent families, in family day care homes and child care centers in Victoria, B.C.

The five studies thus were roughly comparable, or at least overlapped in sample size and age of subjects. All studies included children in centers; the Victoria Study and the Chicago Study each also included a comparison group of children in family day care homes. The majority of children in all the studies were in child care close to full-time and had been there for some time (usually at least 6 months); however time in child care ranged substantially *within* studies. The quality of the child care programs varied within each study — not surprisingly, as this was the focus of investigation in these projects — but the range was apparently more restricted and narrow in some research (Kontos and Fiene's) than in other research (Phillips et al.).

In terms of family characteristics, each researcher included a range of socioeconomic backgrounds, except Howes, whose subjects were all middle-class. In the Chicago Study, we selected only self-supporting families, so our sample was biased toward the upper end of the socioeconomic range. Unfortunately, the proportions of lower- and middle-class families in the other studies were not usually reported, so it is hard to make comparisons across studies on SES distributions. Each study apparently included both single parent and two-parent families, except the Chicago Study, for which we selected only two-parent families. There were also different proportions of Black and White families.

The most obvious difference among the studies was their locations. The five studies were done in places as varied as Bermuda, to Victoria, northeastern Pennsylvania, Chicago, and Los Angeles — each with its own regional distinctions. The effects of the differences in location on either child care or children's development are of unknown significance.

Caregiver behavior that is verbal, stimulating, educational, and not demeaning to the child appears to facilitate child development.

Although the five studies were in many ways comparable, there were significant differences in their locations and samples. This suggests that one way to explain inconsistencies in results is to look to differences among the samples.

Another way we might explain inconsistencies is to point to differences in the methods and measures used in the different studies. In the five studies, measures were overlapping but not identical. In each study, there were three categories of variables: child development variables, child care quality variables, and family background variables.

1. In the category of child development variables, all the investigators obtained some measure of children's language or intellectual development (using standard tests like the Peabody Picture Vocabulary Test or made-up ones like the assessments we did in the Chicago Study on conceptual perspective taking) and/or some measure of children's social competence or adjustment (using teacher ratings or observed behavior in laboratory situations).

2. In the category of child care quality variables, three investigators included measures of the child care setting (home versus center); most included some measure of overall child care quality (the Harms and Clifford ECERS was used by three); most included measures of observed interactions between children and caregivers or among children; and all included indexes of some policy-regulable variables (most commonly, adult-child ratio, caregiver training, caregiver experience, caregiver stability, and group size).

3. In the category of family background variables, most researchers included demographic variables (e.g., family structure, SES, parental education), some observation of home stimulation (such as the HOME scale), and some measure of parental attitudes or values.

Despite the overlap in *categories* assessed, though, there are enough differences among studies in the *specific* measures used to account for some inconsistencies among results.

Keeping these differences—in samples and in measures—in mind, just how consistent were the results of the five different studies? To consider this question, I have divided the results into five different areas: results related to the effects of (1) the child care setting, (2) children's interactive experiences in the child care setting, (3) the overall quality of the child care program, (4) policy-regulable variables, and (5) family background variables.

Across a variety of child development measures, children in center programs did better than children in homes.

Child care setting

Child care settings (home and center) were examined by Goelman and Pence, Howes, and our Chicago Study—with, happily, some consistency of results. Across a variety of child development measures (language, intelligence, social competence, independence) children in center programs did better than children in homes (in their own homes with mother or caregiver, or in unlicensed family day care homes).

For example, in the Chicago Study, children in centers, either part-time or full-time, were 6 to 9 months more advanced than children in homes on measures of social and intellectual competence. In Goelman and Pence's study, children in licensed day care homes did as well on measures of language development as children in licensed centers. Perhaps these differences are the result of licensed facilities' more explicit educational programs, licensed caregivers' greater sense of professional commitment, or the more stimulating activities and interactions that children in licensed programs experience.

To test these possibilities, both Goelman and Pence and we in Chicago compared observations of children's activities in different child care settings. In the Chicago Study we found that children in centers, as contrasted to children in unlicensed homes, spent more time in group activities (including formal lessons with the teacher, singing, and being read to) and spent less time watching TV and playing with an adult. Children's experiences in center programs were more structured than in home care arrangements and more likely to be guided by an explicit educational curriculum. These differences seem reasonable as predictors of the advanced development observed in center children.

Goelman and Pence found some similar differences. Center children engaged in more informational activities and less television watching than children in homes. I suspect that Goelman and Pence did not find the other curriculum differences we observed because they did their observations only during free play periods, thus eliminating the structured activities we found to discriminate between home and center settings.

More important for understanding child care quality than any lack of consistency between these two studies, though, is whether the activities that we found to discriminate between centers and homes were related to individual children's development. We turn to this possibility next.

Interactions in child care

Although children's interactions with caregivers were observed in four of the five studies, correlations with child development were reported for only two (Bermuda and Chicago). In the Chicago Study, we found that in family day care homes children's social and cognitive development was positively related to the amount the caregiver talked to, touched, read to, and directed the child, negatively related to the amount the caregiver helped the child, and unrelated to the amount the caregiver hugged, played with, taught, or offered choices to the child. In centers, children's social and cognitive development was positively related to the amount the caregiver read and offered choices to the child, negatively related to the amount the caregiver hugged, held, helped, directed, and controlled the child, and unrelated to the amount the caregiver talked to, taught, or played with the child. The Bermuda researchers reported only correlations with the amount the caregiver talked to the child, and they found that this variable was significantly related to children's social and cognitive development in centers (as we had found in homes but not in centers). To explain this difference, I have two suggestions: First, the Bermuda group may have observed either a greater range of variation in the amount caregivers talked or caregivers from the low end of the range of caregiver talking than we did. A larger range is more likely to produce a statistically significant correlation than a smaller range.

Second, utterances from caregivers may be functionally different in different kinds of child care. Perhaps child care center programs in Bermuda are more informal and less academic than center programs in Chicago and so are more like American family day care *homes* (in which the amount of caregiver talk *was* related to children's development). To resolve this question, other researchers should analyze correlations between caregiver talk and child development in their studies. For now, on the basis of both the Bermuda and the Chicago studies, it looks as if the amount of caregiver behavior that is verbal, stimulating, educational, and not demeaning to the child (controlling, helping, or holding) positively predicts child development — as long as a wide enough range is sampled.

Children's interaction with their peers in child care also was observed and analyzed in the Bermuda (McCartney, 1984, 1986) and Chicago studies. The results of the two studies are consistent in suggesting that too much time spent interacting with other children may be detrimental to children's development, but they differ on the details. In the Chicago Study, we found that in both homes and centers children who spent more of their time watching, playing with, fighting with, or imitating other children, especially if the other children were younger, were less socially competent in our laboratory assessment of sociability and cooperation with adult and child strangers and less independent of their mothers. Consistent with this, Phillips, Scarr, and McCartney also found a relation between more frequent peer interaction in child care and children's dependency, anxiety, aggression, and low task orientation. They used verbal interaction as a measure of peer interaction; we did not find that particular measure of peer interaction to be significantly correlated with measures of child competence, but at least there is thematic consistency.

Inconsistent with our results, however, the Bermuda researchers found that more frequent interaction with peers was related to children's higher sociability. The reason for this difference between studies, I suspect, is the difference in measurement. In the Bermuda Study, the measure of children's sociability was a rating made by the child's caregiver; it was not an independent assessment. Because caregivers would base their rating of children's sociability on the social behavior they observed in the classroom, the relation is tautological: Children who interacted more with other children in the classroom would be rated as more sociable by their teachers. In the Chicago Study our measure of sociability was one that, obtained in the laboratory, not only was independent of classroom behavior, but involved unfamiliar peers rather than the child's friends and reflected qualitative not quantitative differences in social behavior. With only these two studies — in Bermuda and Chicago — then, we have consistent results that suggest that child care programs in which children are left to spend a major part of their time interacting with other children, rather than hearing a story or engaging in a more structured activity planned by an adult caregiver, are unlikely to benefit children's development.

Child care quality measures

The next area of results in the five studies was the overall quality of child care. The most commonly used index of overall quality was the Harms and Clifford Early Childhood Environment Rating Scale (ECERS). This scale consists of 37 items forming seven subscales (personal care routines, furnishings/display, language/reasoning activities, creative activities, fine and gross motor activities, social development, and adult/staff needs), which can be summed to give an overall index of quality. Three of the five studies (Victoria, Bermuda, and Pennsylvania) included this scale. The results were surprisingly *in*consistent: Phillips, Scarr and McCartney found the ECERS to be positively related to the social competence, intelligence, and language of children in centers; Kontos and Fiene found the Scale to be negatively related to the social competence and language of children in centers; Goelman and Pence found a similar home rating scale devised by Harms and Clifford (DCHERS) to be positively related to the intelligence and language of children in family day care homes, but the ECERS was not related to the intelligence and language of children in centers in their study.

Why the inconsistencies? Several explanations are possible. First, we may be able to explain the particular inconsistency between the Victoria and Bermuda studies because Goelman and Pence had a greater range of variation among their family day care homes than among their child care centers, and the DCHERS/ECERS was positively related to positive caregiver behaviors (reading, informing) in the homes but negatively related in the centers.

Second, and more importantly however, an explanation of inconsistencies involves the ECERS itself. This scale was made up from experts' suggestions about what constitutes good child care. Its items and its subscales were not empirically based or empirically weighted. Hence equal weight is given to disparate items. Also, because in the ECERS the researcher simply adds up items to get the overall index of quality, different subscales are weighted arbitrarily by the number of items each contains. Therefore, the ECERS may be useful for selecting a high quality child care center to send children to, but it is not useful for research purposes, when we are searching for differentiated predictors of particular child development outcomes.

This raises a more general problem. The ECERS aside, why should we expect *any* overall index of quality to be predictive of children's development in child care? One center might get an excellent rating for the academic items on the index; another center might be excellent for the socioemotional items. The two centers would get identical scores on the overall index. But children in the first center might be expected to do better on tests of academic performance, whereas children in the second center would be expected to do better on assessments of socioemotional adjustment. A global index of quality *masks* effects of different program components. Different programs have different strengths and weaknesses, and it is unlikely that any program can be all things to all children. (Remember those children from the Frank Porter Graham Center [Haskins, 1985], who were very intelligent but also 13 times more aggressive than children who had not attended that intellectually stimulating program!)

Kontos and Fiene demonstrated that different indexes of quality (the ECERS, the Pennsylvania Licensing Questionnaire, and the measures of regulatory variables), were not intercorrelated. But is this surprising? Calling something *quality* does not make it equivalent to something else that is also called *quality*, if one is the quality of educational materials and the other refers for example, to physical characteristics of the program. And having high quality of one does not necessarily mean that there will be high quality of the other in any particular center. Having both developmentally appropriate instruction and excellent physical space may reflect high quality, but they do not necessarily co-occur; a director may choose to put the inevitably limited program resources into one *or* the other.

For research purposes, an alternative way of thinking about child care quality is to define different aspects of quality in terms of their empirical prediction of advanced child development. This does not mean that factors that do *not* predict differences in child development are not important aspects of quality. Physical safety factors, for example, *may* not predict advanced child development, but it only takes one child falling down the stairs to remind us that they are an essential part of a high quality program. Nevertheless, taking the empirical prediction approach can be useful for finding out about quality. In the Chicago Study, we discovered that the qualities that predicted good child development, in centers and family day care homes, were the following:

- a neat, clean, orderly physical setting organized into activity areas and oriented to the child's activity;

- a caregiver whose interactions with the child were responsive, accepting, and informative; and

- classmates who were older and more mature and so could set a good example for the child.

These links seem sensible, but they need empirical corrobation from other research.

We should avoid blanket statements about high adult-child ratios being good and low ratios being bad until we check out

Regulable variables

The next area of results included in the five studies was findings related to those variables that are regulable by policy — adult-child ratio, caregiver training, class size, and so on. These are well-established, time-honored measures in child care research. But even for these variables, the consensus among the five studies was underwhelming.

First, the results of analyses correlating adult-child ratios with child development were inconsistent. Phillips and her colleagues found that a high adult-child ratio in the group correlated with children's social competence, and so did Howes (at least in combination with caregiver training and stability). But in the Chicago Study we found the reverse: A high adult-child ratio was related to lower social competence. Why? Perhaps the inconsistency lies in the difference between the measures of competence. In the Los Angeles and Bermuda studies, social competence was measured in terms of children's considerateness, compliance, and independence. In the Chicago Study, social competence was measured in terms of children's sociability, cooperation, and positive behavior with unfamiliar children and adults. Perhaps the inconsistency resulted from the different ranges of adult-child ratios represented in the studies (both Howes and Phillips et al. had wider ranges than we did in Chicago), or from the different sections of the range sampled (their studies included more low quality care than ours, and so, perhaps, worse adult-child ratios). Whichever explanation is correct, these results suggest that we should avoid simple blanket statements about high adult-child ratios being good and low ratios being bad until we have checked out the *limits* beyond which a low ratio is bad and the *outcome* for which a high ratio is good.

The second regulable variable studied was caregiver experience. Here, too, results were inconsistent. In the Pennsylvania Study, children in programs with more experienced directors did better on measures of language and sociability; in the Bermuda Study children with more experienced directors did better on measures of social adjustment (less aggressive, anxious, and hyperactive) but worse on measures of sociability. Why? One possibility, again, is that the two studies tapped different parts of the range of caregiver experience. Kontos and Fiene reported a range of 2 to 14 years experience; Phillips et al. reported a range of 11 to 25 years. It appears likely that the relation between caregiver experience and child development is curvilinear, with an optimal level, perhaps, falling between 10 and 15 years. We could also query whether more experienced directors *the* limits *beyond which a low ratio is bad and the* outcome *for which a high ratio is good.*

---

in Pennsylvania and Bermuda were equivalent in ideology, attitudes, and so on. Kontos and Fiene, and Phillips, Scarr, and McCartney, did not report the ages of the caregivers. However in the Chicago Study we found that children with older caregivers had high cognitive competence but low sociability. The need for further examination of the data collected in the five studies is clear.

The third regulable variable analyzed in the five studies was caregiver stability. It is hard to compare results across studies because the Pennsylvania and Bermuda measure of caregiver stability was percent turnover, the Los Angeles measure was number of new caregivers in the center during the last year, and our measure was the length of time the caregiver had been in the center. Nevertheless, some consistency did appear. In Pennsylvania and Chicago there was a positive relation between caregiver stability and children's social and intellectual development; in Bermuda, high caregiver stability was related to better social adjustment (children were less anxious and dependent), and in Los Angeles caregiver stability was included in the index of quality that predicted children's social competence. Unfortunately, in the Pennsylvania study, the relation was not statistically significant; in the Los Angeles study, a separate correlation for caregiver stability was not reported; and in the Bermuda study, high caregiver stability was related to low scores on intellectual assessments. There are only inconsistent hints that caregiver stability is somewhat positively related to child development.

The fourth regulable variable was caregiver education and training. There is some faint glimmer of consistency here, but not as strong as one might hope or expect. In both Victoria and Chicago, caregiver training in child development was significantly related to children's intellectual and language development—although Goelman and Pence found the relation significant only in family day care homes, and we found it significant only in child care centers. But, as I mentioned before, this is probably the result of the relative variation in our samples: Goelman and Pence had more variation in their family day care home sample, and we had more variation in our center sample. However, in the Chicago Study, we found that children with more highly trained caregivers also did more poorly in our assessments of *social* competence. It was children who had caregivers with higher levels of education (i.e., college graduates) rather than more formal training in child development who did better socially. This suggests that, for our sample of caregivers at least, formal academic training in child development may have emphasized the importance of preparing children academically at the expense of their social skills. We need to

Formal training in child development may emphasize the importance of preparing children academically at the expense of their social skills.

investigate the effects of specific kinds of caregiver training, not just the number of courses taken.

Finally, the last regulable variable studied was group size. Once again, relations with child development were disappointingly weak. Small group size in centers was related to some positive outcomes for children in Pennsylvania and Chicago. For Kontos and Fiene, it was language and intelligence; for us it was social competence. But their correlation, although statistically significant, was small, and we found that children in small classes, although they were more friendly and cooperative with strangers, did more poorly on measures of social cognition. Suffice it to say, the picture is not entirely clear even on this supposed *sine qua non* of good quality child care.

Although regulable variables may be (as Kontos and Fiene report) more predictive of child development than are overall quality measures — especially if they are clustered together to increase the percent of the variance accounted for — they clearly leave something to be desired in terms of consistency and absolute significance. They may be more predictive than other measures we have discussed simply because they are easily quantified and we can assess them more reliably. But they are still relatively weak and not very consistent in their effects. This is not to say that they are not important. We need to examine the limits beyond which each variable makes a meaningful difference for children's development and not just continue our search for statistically significant correlations. I would guess that detrimental effects of extremely *low* scores on measures of regulable variables would be stronger and more meaningful than the beneficial effects of extremely *high* scores, for instance. If this were the case, we might not want to invest too much effort in increasing adult-child ratios or decreasing class size far beyond the levels recommended by state and local authorities, but rather work at making sure that *all* child care facilities meet these minimal standards. This suggestion needs to be explored empirically and experimentally.

Family variables

The last area of results for the five studies involves the significance of family background variables. A number of researchers have recently discovered that even though children are in child care for 40 hours a week or more, the influence of their families, whether by nature or by nurture,

We might want to invest our efforts into making sure that all child care meets minimal standards.

does not go away. The studies in this monograph provide evidence that children's development (especially their cognitive and language development) is directly linked to their family structure, SES, home stimulation, and parental values. These links have been demonstrated many times before for children who are *not* in child care. Perhaps the surprising thing is that the links are still there when children *are* in child care. Even more surprising, the links are sometimes stronger than the links observed between child development and child care variables. This was seen, for example, in Kontos and Fiene's study: When child care and family variables were pitted against each other in regression analyses predicting child development, the family factors were more highly predictive.

This evidence of links between family factors and child development measures suggests that one way families influence their children's development is through simple direct effects that are unaffected by participation in child care. But there are other ways in which families may influence their children's development. One additional possibility is through their *additive* contribution when combined with children's child care experiences. Investigators who have done the relevant analyses, such as Howes and us, have found that combining home and child care variables is more predictive of child development than using either alone. For example, in the Chicago Study, summing up the number of different kinds of toys in both home and child care settings or using both home and child care measures of the number of different kinds of toys in a regression analysis was more predictive of children's development than using either alone (Clarke-Stewart, 1984).

Another possibility is *interactive* effects between children's experiences at home and in child care, so that, for instance, high cognitive scores might be observed for children whose families were low in educational stimulation but whose child care centers were high in educational stimulation. No such interactions were reported here, however.

A further possibility is that children's development would benefit if the child's family and child care situations were *similar*. For example, children would do well when both their parents and their daytime caregivers shared the same ideas about discipline (both strict or both lax). Again, none of the investigators here reported such effects. In the Chicago Study (Clarke-Stewart, 1984) an elaborately constructed measure of the mesh between family and child care features—similarity in ethnicity, values, SES, and age, for example—yielded no meaningful correlations with child development. But this possibility bears further investigation.

Finally, there is the possibility that families influence children's development because family and child care variables are *correlated*. Parents are selective in choosing child care for their children, and more stimulating parents choose more stimulating programs. The studies in this monograph touch on this question and provide some evidence that such selection does occur. In Victoria, married and highly educated mothers chose high quality child care. In Los Angeles, parents who felt in control of their children chose high quality child care. In the Chicago Study, parents who valued education chose high quality nursery school programs. In Bermuda, parents who placed a higher value on the development of social skills and a lower value on encouraging conformity were found to select higher quality child care centers. In Pennsylvania, where poor families had the benefit of high quality child care because it was subsidized by the state, did such selection not occur. Ordinarily, self-selection probably does occur, and we must watch out for the confounding of family background and child care variables and not infer that observed correlations represent direct effects of child care *alone*. This does not mean that we should try to eliminate the natural correlation between family characteristics and child care characteristics in our studies (unless we are doing experiments) — or we may all get misleading correlations like the negative correlation between child care quality and child development identified in the Pennsylvania Study. It does mean that we need to contain our claims about child care effects.

To sum up this discussion — simplifying to the point of oversimplifying — we can say that on the basis of these five studies the best predictors of advanced child development, and hence our best clues as to indexes of quality child care, are the following:

- a licensed program (usually in a center)
- in which the child's interaction with the caregiver is frequent, verbal, and educational, rather than custodial and controlling;
- in which children are not left to spend their time in aimless play together;
- in which there is an adequate adult-child ratio (for older preschoolers, probably not lower than 1:12) and a reasonable group size (probably not larger than 25); and
- in which the caregiver has a balanced training in child development, some degree of professional experience in child care, and has been in the program for some period of time.

We must watch out for the confounding of family background and child care variables.

Although these variables are related to advanced child development, it is important to reiterate that we do not have evidence that they *alone* are causing advanced development. Children are most advanced when their experiences both at home and in care are stimulating.

In conclusion, let me suggest that to proceed in our search for predictors of high quality child care, we need to carefully select our measures and analyses. Clarity and consistency may be out there, but we can see them, if at all, only through a wave darkly. There are many apparent inconsistencies in the results of our research—the consequence of different samples, different measures, unknown sources of variation, and random events. We should not be discouraged by this. We would be expecting too much of our primitive methods if we expected a completely clear picture at this point.

As researchers we must fine tune our research strategies. For one thing, we need to do more nonlinear analyses, looking for curvilinear relations. Perhaps for some child care quality variables, some quantity is necessary, like the minimum daily requirement of vitamin A, but more is not better and, in fact, beyond a certain point, may be worse.

We also need to do more subanalyses with identical measures and statistical procedures for different samples, within different ranges, in different family types. We must continue our efforts to put our measures together in multivariate analyses and regression equations. Most important, perhaps, whenever possible, we should seize opportunities to carry out experiments, comparing children's progress in different kinds of groups to which they have been randomly assigned. Research on child care is difficult, time consuming, and expensive—often overwhelmingly so. It demands our continued concern and concentration. But if we continue with the kind of research described in this monograph and extend it carefully and systematically, we may avoid drowning in the third wave of research as we push forward in our never-ending search for predictors of high quality child care.

As researchers we must fine tune our research strategies.

References

Clarke-Stewart, K.A. (1984). Day care: A new context for research and development. In M. Perlmutter (Ed.), *The Minnesota Symposium on Child Psychology* (Vol. 17). Hillsdale, NJ: Erlbaum.

Haskins, R. (1985). Public aggression among children with varying day-care experience. *Child Development, 57,* 698–703.

McCartney, K. (1984). The effect of quality day care environment upon young children's language development. *Developmental Psychology, 20,* 249–260.

Epilogue

Deborah A. Phillips

WHERE DO we go from here? We have answered some questions and left many others unanswered. We have also approached some enduring issues from new vantage points and revealed new questions. As the questions have evolved, the field has acquired increasing sophistication about *how* to put its finger on the pulse of quality in child care. In this monograph, we have examined studies from wave 3 of child care research. What are the challenges that face wave 4? With this question in mind, we conclude with some thoughts about new territory for future research.

Quality as configuration

Perhaps the goal of identifying key ingredients of high quality child care is unattainable. The research in this volume demonstrates that good things go together in child care. Child care *in the community* does not offer researchers the opportunity to isolate staff-child ratios or staff training from other predictors of good quality care. This fact deserves our attention and prompts a shift in how we approach the task of defining quality child care.

Quality may be most appropriately understood and studied as a blend or configuration of ingredients. Excellent ratios in the absence of trained staff and parent participation may have minimal effects on program quality. Conversely, the positive effects of excellent ratios may be compounded in programs with trained staff and ample parent involvement. These interactive effects and clusters of quality indicators that occur in the real world of child care constitute relatively uncharted territory for researchers.

The work environment of child care

Child care has been studied largely as a developmental environment for young children. This is understandable in light of the history of concern about the developmental effects of child care. Child care has also been studied, primarily by economists and sociologists, as a factor that predicts maternal labor force participation and childbearing (Blau & Robins, 1986; Presser & Baldwin, 1980).

Although the preponderance of research evidence has ascribed positive developmental outcomes for children in child care to trained and stable staff, the role of child care as a work environment for adults remains virtually unstudied. This outcome stands in stark contrast to national statistics that reveal a 42% annual turnover rate among child care workers and to anecdotal reports of severe shortages of trained adults to replace those who have left the field.

Low pay, lack of benefits, and stressful working conditions are the major reasons reported by child care workers for their high turnover rate (Jorde-Bloom, 1987; Kontos & Stremmel, 1987; Whitebook, Howes, Friedman, & Darrah, 1982). But little is known about factors that affect staff turnover, about the association between training and turnover, and about how these associations vary with caregiver characteristics and features of child care.

Important questions include: (1) What factors in child care and in caregivers predict job satisfaction? (2) Do these predictive relations vary with the type, quality, and auspices of the child care program, or with the ages of the children in care? (3) What is the relation between job satisfaction, caregiver behavior, and career commitment? (4) What are the relations among these features of the work or adult environment, the developmental environment of child care, and children's actual development in child care?

Capturing the real range of child care quality

Although the calls to move child care research beyond high quality university-based centers have been heeded, substantial room for improvement remains. Each of the studies presented in this volume examined nonoptimal child care as part of assessing a range of quality. The Victoria Study (Goelman & Pence, this volume) even included unregulated family day care homes in its sample. But studies of this type are all too rare.

Child care consists largely of unregulated arrangements. Pressures at the federal policy level threaten to expand the supply of child care without regard to regulation or quality. Many states retain numerous exemptions from regulations for church-run, part-day, or state-sponsored child care programs. And the unrelenting demand for relatively scarce forms of licensed care, such as center-based care for infants, implies that more children will be placed in nonpreferred arrangements while on waiting lists for the parents' program of choice.

In light of these trends, it is essential that deliberate steps be taken to include low quality and unregulated arrangements (which are not necessarily low in quality) in future studies of child care. Concluding that high quality child care is good for children has a flip side. But until we can describe more fully the negative consequences of poor child care, this issue remains largely an abstraction, and policies that trade off quality to expand the supply of child care will persist.

Multisite studies

Regulations, exemptions, and thus the broad parameters that determine quality of child care vary widely from state to state. With the notable exception of the National Day Care Study, however, child care research has been restricted to single site (and often single program) investigations that fail to reflect national diversity in the child care market. This, in turn, compromises the generalizability of research results and restricts the policy relevance of much child care research. For example, stringent regulations in some states, such as Massachusetts, would be expected to elevate the quality of typical care, but also to increase costs to working parents relative to costs in other states.

Similarly, regional variation in economic conditions would be expected to affect both the home and child care environments to which children are exposed. Our research on child care is an essentially urban literature, with a few examples of suburban studies. Rural child care is an unknown quantity although two rural centers were included in the Pennsylvania study.

Until we incorporate state and regional variation in studies of child care, the generalizability and policy significance of our results will be circumscribed. The challenges here are largely practical. Multisite studies are time consuming and expensive. But without them we run the risk of overlooking some important factors in the search for indicators of high quality child care.

Child care as part of a collaboration

From the child's viewpoint, child care is a joint enterprise of parents and caregivers. This fact is partially recognized in studies, such as those in this volume, that examine the joint effects of home and child care environments on child development. There is, however, one facet of this issue that has received scant attention, namely parent-caregiver relations. Even less studied are the effects on parents of child care programs not designed as early intervention.

Powell (1977, 1980) first raised the question of the social distance between parents and caregivers, and Peters and his colleagues (Long, Peters, & Garduque, 1985; Peters & Benn, 1980) have extended this question to the broader issue of home-child care continuity. The ensuing research (Galinsky, 1986; Kontos, 1984) has revealed that many caregivers harbor negative attitudes toward the parents whose children are in their care. Kontos and Wells (1986) have further revealed that these attitudes vary with the caregivers' perceptions of the quality of parental childrearing (including patience and authoritarianism), maternal education, parental marital status, and whether the parents are using subsidized care.

With respect to the quality of child care, this emerging literature raises significant questions about whether caregiver attitudes affect the socioemotional quality of children's child care environments, and, in turn, the developmental effects of child care. Kontos and Wells's preliminary data suggest that children's experiences in child care vary little as a function of caregiver attitudes toward parents. But many important questions remain: (1) What is the association between parent-caregiver relations and caregiver-child interactions, particularly at entry and departure times? (2) Is tension transmitted to the child, and how does this affect the child's adjustment to child care? (3) What are the relative effects on child development of program quality as measured by objective observations and by caregiver and parent perceptions of the child care experience?

Longitudinal data

Unlike research on early intervention programs, the child care literature is devoid of longitudinal studies. While understandable in light of the long-term policy goals of early intervention and the more immediate employment-related goals of child care (Phillips & Zigler, 1987), this gap has nonetheless fueled perceptions of child care as nondevelopmental and noneducational, and impeded efforts to advocate for higher quality care. In the early childhood area, sustained financial support seems to follow evidence of sustained benefits.

A particularly fruitful time frame for longitudinal studies of child care would involve following children across the transition from child care to formal schooling. The critical issue is whether high quality child care serves to launch children on a trajectory of school success, thus maximizing the return on the more expensive child care investment. A second step would involve identifying those processes that function to sustain benefits (see Aber, Molnar, & Phillips, 1986).

Conclusion

In a hearing held by Senator Christopher Dodd as chair of the Subcommittee on Children, Families, Drugs and Alcoholism (U.S. Senate, June 11, 1987), Edward Zigler portrayed family day care as a "cosmic crapshoot," a detective in the Miami Police Department described the tragic death of two children subjected to patchwork child care while their mother waited for a licensed space, and Caro Pemberton from the Child Care Employee Project reported the 42% annual turnover rate among child care staff.

At the outset of this volume, I portrayed quality as the luxury issue in child care. These witnesses before the U.S. Congress testified to the consequences of this mentality.

Research is one important cog in a chain of events that can stretch the limits of what is considered possible and what is considered essential for the well-being of this nation's children and families. It is our hope that this volume and the new research directions that it points to will serve this purpose.

References

Aber, L., Molnar, J., & Phillips, D. (1986, December). *Action research in early education: A role for the philanthropic and research communities in the New York City initiative for four-year-olds*. Report prepared for the Foundation for Child Development, New York, New York.

Blau, D.M., & Robins, P.K. (1986, October). *Fertility, employment, and child care*. Report to the Department of Health and Human Services, National Institute of Child Health and Human Development, Washington, D.C.

Galinsky, E. (1986). Contemporary patterns of child care. In N. Gunzenhauser & B. D. Caldwell (Eds.), *Group care for young children*. Skillman, NJ: Johnson & Johnson.

Jorde-Bloom, P. (April, 1987). *Factors influencing overall job commitment and facet satisfaction in early childhood work environments*. Paper presented at the meetings of the American Educational Research Association, Washington, D.C.

Kontos, S. (1984). Congruence of parent and early childhood staff perceptions of parenting. *Parenting Studies, 1,* 5–10.

Kontos, S., & Stremmel, A.J. (1987). *Caregivers' perceptions of working conditions in a child care environment*. Manuscript submitted for publication.

Kontos, S., & Wells, W. (1986). Attitudes of caregivers and the day care experiences of families. *Early Childhood Research Quarterly, 1,* 47–67.

Long, R., Peters, D.L., & Garduque, L. (1985). Continuity between home and day care: A model for defining relevant dimensions of child care. In I. Sigel (Ed.), *Advances in applied developmental psychology* (Vol. 1). Norwood, NJ: Ablex.

Peters, D., & Benn, J. (1980). Day care: Support for the family. *Dimensions, 9,* 78–82.

Phillips, D., & Zigler, E. (1987). The checkered history of federal child care regulation. In E. Rothkopf (Ed.), *Review of research in education* (Vol. 14). Washington, DC: American Education Research Association.

Powell, D. (1977). *The interface between families and childcare programs: A study of parent-caregiver relationships.* Detroit: Merrill-Palmer Institute.

Powell, D. (1980). Toward a sociological perspective of relations between parents and child care programs. In S.J. Kilmer (Ed.), *Advances in early education and day care* (Vol. 1) (pp. 203–226). Greenwich, CT: JAI Press.

Presser, H.B., & Baldwin, W. (1980). Child care as a constraint on employment: Prevalence, correlates, and bearing on the work and fertility nexus. *American Journal of Sociology, 85,* 1202–1213.

U.S. Senate, Subcommittee on Children, Families, Drugs and Alcoholism. (June 11, 1987). *Hearing record on child care.* Washington, DC: U.S. Senate.

Whitebook, M., Howes, C., Friedman, J., & Darrah, R. (1982). Caring for the caregivers: Burn-out in child care. In L. Katz (Ed.), *Current topics in early childhood education* (Vol. 4). Norwood, NJ: Ablex.

Subject Index

Adaptive Language Inventory (ALI) 46, 47, 49, 51, 63, 70, 75
Adult-child ratios x, 2, 3, 4, 5, 8, 10, 22, 23, 28, 30, 35, 36, 37, 38, 39, 44, 45, 46, 49, 50, 51, 53, 54, 61, 62, 65, 76, 81-82, 84, 86, 87, 108, 114, 116, 119
Bermuda Study ix, 4, 9, 10, 43-54, 57, 63, 76, 100, 106, 110, 111, 112, 114, 115
CDPE Indicator Checklist (CDPE-IC) 61, 62, 64, 65, 67
Caregiver Observation Form and Scale (COFAS) 61, 62, 64, 65, 67, 77
Caregiver characteristics (See also Caregiver experience, Caregiver training) 3, 34, 36, 38, 89, 90
Caregiver experience 5, 6, 7, 8, 27, 28, 29, 47, 54, 62, 70, 75, 76, 93, 108, 114, 119
Caregiver stability x, 3, 4, 10-11, 44, 45, 46, 49, 50, 51, 53, 54, 62, 67, 72, 76, 81, 82, 84, 87, 108, 114, 115
Caregiver training x, 2, 3, 4, 5, 6, 7, 10, 22, 24, 27, 28, 29, 36, 44, 45, 81, 82-83, 84, 87, 93, 99, 108, 114, 115, 116, 119
Center child care ix, 9, 10, 11, 13, 14, 22, 23, 29-30, 89, 90
Chicago Study of Child Care and Development ix, 10, 13, 21-41, 106, 109, 110, 111, 113, 114, 115, 116, 117, 118
Child Development Program Evaluation Scale (CDPE) 61, 64, 65
Child Observation Form (COF) 93, 94, 96
Child's child care experience ix, 50, 53, 67, 70, 85, 89, 93, 116
Children's Behavior Questionnaire 63
Classroom Behavior Inventory 46, 63, 70, 72, 75
Day Care Home Environment Rating Scale (DCHERS) 93, 94, 96, 97, 112
Day Care Environment Inventory 46
Director experience 44, 45, 46, 49, 50, 51, 53, 62, 67, 72, 75, 76, 114, 115
Early Childhood Environment Rating Scale (ECERS) 4, 46, 47, 49, 50, 51, 61, 62, 64, 65, 70, 72, 76, 92, 93, 94, 96, 97, 98, 100, 108, 111, 112, 113
Expressive One-Word Picture Vocabulary Test (EOWPVT) 90, 97, 98, 100
Family variables ix, 3, 11, 12, 14, 15, 23-24, 43, 45, 46-47, 50, 53, 63-64, 67, 68, 70, 72, 75, 76, 77, 83, 84, 85-86, 92, 99, 101, 102, 108, 117-118

Family day care ix, 9, 10, 11, 13, 14, 21, 22, 23, 25, 27-28, 34-35, 89, 90
Forms of child care (See also In-home care, Family day care, Child care centers, Nursery schools) ix, 3, 9-10, 13, 22, 30-33, 89, 90, 109
Frank Porter Graham Center 113
Griffiths Scale of Mental Development 13
Group size 2, 3, 6, 10, 22, 25, 28, 29, 34, 35, 36, 39, 62, 65, 72, 75, 108, 114, 116, 119
HOME Inventory 64, 108
Home environments x, 13, 64
In-home care ix, 9, 10, 11, 13, 22, 23, 24-25
Infants and toddlers x, 2, 4, 6, 8, 11, 14, 54, 81
Language development x, 4, 8, 9, 10, 43, 47, 49, 50, 51, 53, 54, 57, 62, 67, 68, 70, 72, 75, 76, 89, 115
Los Angeles Study 81-88, 106, 114, 115, 118
National Day Care Study 1, 2, 3, 5, 6, 7, 8, 37, 54, 70, 76, 123
National Opinion Research Corporation Prestige Scale 45
Nursery schools ix, 10, 21, 22, 23, 28-29
Office of Children, Youth and Families 58, 61
One-to-one interaction 25, 29
Preschool Language Assessment Instrument (PLAI) 46, 47, 50, 51, 53
Peabody Picture Vocabulary Test (PPVT) 46, 47, 49, 50, 51, 53, 90, 96, 97, 98, 100, 108
Parent as Educator Interview 46, 64
Pearson Product-Moment 67, 70
Pennsylvania Day Care Study ix, 57-79, 106, 112, 113, 114, 115, 116, 118
Pennsylvania Licensing Questionnaire 113
Physical setting 24, 35, 37, 39
Play 94-96
Preschool Behavior Questionnaire 46, 49, 63, 67
Slosson Intelligence Test, 63, 64, 70, 77
Sociability 31
Social development, 4, 9, 43, 47, 49, 50, 53, 54, 57, 62, 67, 68, 70
Staff turnover. See Caregiver stability
Test of Early Language Development (TELD) 63, 64, 67, 70, 72, 77
Television 30, 35, 96, 99, 100, 109
Victoria Day Care Research Project x, 89-103, 106, 112, 115, 118

Author Index

Aber, L. 124
Ainslie, R.C. 10
Ainsworth, M. 82, 83
Ambron, S.R. 11, 13, 14
Anderson, C.W. 10
Apietz, A.L. See H. L. Bee
Arnett, J. 7

Baldwin, W. 121
Barnard, K.E. See H. L. Bee
Beagles-Ross, J. 6
Bee, H.L. 89
Behar, L. 46, 49, 63
Bell, C. 37
Bell, N.J. 89
Beller, E.K. 37
Belsky, J. 43
Benn, J. 124
Benn, R. 9, 10, 11
Berk, L. 7
Berlin, L.J. 46
Blank, M. 46
Blau, D.M. 121
Blehar, M. 82, 83
Boyle, P. 8, 83
Bradley, R. 64
Brownlee, M. See M. Golden
Bruner, J. 6
Brush, L.R. See S. Fosburg
Burchinal, M. 10

Caldwell, B. 64
Carew, J.V. 8, 102
Carmichael, H. 37
Charlesworth, M. 90
Clark, B. See H. L. Bee
Clarke-Stewart, K.A. (See also The Chicago Study) ix, x, 1, 6, 7, 9, 10, 12, 13, 21, 22, 31, 35, 43, 76, 83, 90, 100, 105, 117, 118
Clifford, R.M. (See also ECERS) 4, 46, 61, 62, 92, 93, 108, 111
Cochran, M.M. 13
Coelen, C. (See also National Day Care Study, R. Ruopp) 1, 8, 37, 43, 53, 54, 93
Connolly, K.J. 6, 37
Cox, M. 89
Cox, R. 89
Cross, T. 102
Crowell, D. 35
Cummings, E.H. 10
Cummings, M. 6

Dalgleish, M. 37
Darrah, R. 82, 122
Davis, A.J. 6
DeMeis, D. 13, 14

Douglas, E. 61
Dunn, L.M. (See also PPVT) 46, 90
Dyer, J.L. 37

Edgerton, M.D. 46, 63, 64
Ershler, J. 37
Espinosa, L. 35
Estes, D. 89
Everson, M.D. 11, 13, 14
Eyres, S. J. See H. L. Bee

Fargo, J. 35
Farran, D.C. 10, 46, 63
Feagans, L. 46, 63
Fein, G.G. 1, 43
Field, T.M. 5, 6, 37
Fiene, R. (See also The Pennsylvania Study) x, 12, 57, 58, 61, 62, 106, 112, 113, 115, 116, 117
Fosburg, S. 35
Francis, P. 5
Freeman, H. See M. Golden
Friedman, J. 82, 122
Friedrich-Cofer, L.K. 37

Galinsky, E. 124
Gardner, M.F. (See also EOWPVT) 90
Garduque, L. 124
Glantz, F. (See also National Day Care Study, R. Ruopp) 1, 8, 37, 43, 53, 54, 93
Goelman, H. (See also The Victoria Study) x, 12, 89, 90, 92, 93, 106, 109, 112, 115, 116, 122
Golden, M. 8
Goldenberg, C. 85
Golub, J. 85
Goodson, B.D. See S. Fosburg
Gordon, E. 1
Grajek, S. 4, 53, 100
Gray, L.A. See H. L. Bee
Green, C. 87
Grossi, M. See M. Golden
Gruber, C. 6, 7, 9, 10, 12, 22, 31, 76
Gruen, C.E. 35
Gunnarsson, L. 13

Hammill, P.D. 63
Hammond, M.A. See H. L. Bee
Harms, T. (See also ECERS) 4, 46, 61, 62, 92, 93, 108, 111
Haskins, R. 5, 113
Hawkins, P. D. See S. Fosburg
Herzmark, G. 37
Hetherington, E.M. 89
Hock, E. 13, 14
Hofferth, S.L. xi, 9, 81
Howes, C. (See also The Los Angeles

Study) x, 3, 5, 6, 7, 8, 10, 11, 12, 13, 35, 43, 53, 54, 81, 83, 85, 86, 87, 106, 109, 114, 122
Hresko, W. 63
Hughes, M. 102
Huston-Stein, A. 37
Hutaff, S.E. 10

Jencks, C. 75
Johnson, G. 102
Johnson, J.E. 37
Jones, K. 46
Jorde-Bloom, P. 122
Juchnowski, M. 102

Kagan, J. 10, 83
Kagan, M. 35
Katz, L. 83
Kearsley, R.B. 10
Kontos, S. (*See also* The Pennsylvania Study) ix, x, 12, 106, 112, 113, 115, 116, 117, 122, 124
Kopp, C. 83
Kritchevsky, S. 46
Kroh, K. 61

Lamb, M.E. 89
Lee, M. 85
Litwok, E. 37
Long, R. 124

McBride, S. 13, 14
McCartney, K. (*See also* The Bermuda Study, D.A. Phillips, S. Scarr) ix, 4, 9, 11, 12, 46, 49, 53, 57, 62, 76, 100, 106, 110, 111, 112, 115
McGhee, P.E. 89
Miller, L.B. 37
Molnar, J. 124
Morgan, G. 57

National Association for the Education of Young Children 10
Nixon, M. 57, 61, 62

O'Connell, M. 81
Olenick, M. 3, 12, 13, 43, 85, 86, 87

Padan-Belkin, E. 93
Painter, M. 37
Parmenter, G. 102
Pence, A. (*See also* The Victoria Study) x, 12, 89, 90, 92, 93, 106, 109, 112, 115, 116, 122
Peters, D.L. 124
Phillips, D.A. (*See also* The Bermuda Study, K. McCartney, S. Scarr) ix, xi, 4, 9, 11, 12, 49, 53, 54, 57, 76, 81, 100, 106, 111, 112, 114, 115, 121, 124
Philps, J. 37
Pinkerton, G. 37
Plewis, I. 37
Policare, H. *See* M. Golden

Porter, A. 7, 8, 93
Powell, D. 124
Powers, C.P. 3, 4, 53, 76
Prescott, E. 46
Presser, H.B. 121

Ramey, C.T. 5, 10
Rauch, M.D. 35
Reid, D.K. 63
Ricciuti, H. 10
Robins, P.K. 121
Robinson, J. 13
Rogers, C. 81
Rose, S.A. 46
Rosenbluth, L. *See* M. Golden
Roy, C. 37
Rubenstein, J.L. 5, 6, 8, 10, 35, 37, 76, 83
Ruopp, R. 1, 8, 37, 43, 53, 54, 76, 93
Rutter, M. 1, 63

Sarnat, L. 11, 13, 14
Scarr, S. (*See also* The Bermuda Study, K. McCartney, D.A. Phillips) ix, 4, 12, 53, 57, 76, 49, 100, 106, 111, 112, 115
Schaefer, E. 46, 63, 64
Schwarz, J.C. 100
Self, P. 5
Singer, J.D. *See* S. Fosburg
Slosson, R. 63, 72
Smith, J.M. *See* S. Fosburg
Smith, P.K. 5, 6, 37
Snyder, C. *See* H. L. Bee
Stallings, J. 7, 8, 93
Steinberg, L. 43, 87
Stewart, P. 11
Stith, S.M. 6
Stremmel, A. J. 122
Stringfield, S.A. 46, 63
Stuckey, M.F. 89
Sullivan, K. 37
Susman, E.J. 37
Sylva, K. 37

Thompson, R.A. 89
Tizard, B. 37, 102
Travers, J. (*See also* National Day Care Study, R. Ruopp) 1, 8, 37, 43, 53, 93

U.S. Bureau of the Census 9
U.S. Senate Subcommittee on Children, Families, Drugs and Alcoholism 125

Vandell, D.L. 3, 4, 53, 76

Wachs, T.D. 35
Walker, A. 43
Wall, S. 82, 83
Walters, E. 82, 83
Wells, W. 96, 124
Whitebook, M. 82, 122

Zelazo, P.R. 10
Zigler, E. 1, 124, 125

Contributors

K. Alison Clarke-Stewart
PROGRAM IN SOCIAL ECOLOGY
UNIVERSITY OF CALIFORNIA AT IRVINE
IRVINE, CALIFORNIA

Richard Fiene
OFFICE OF CHILDREN, YOUTH AND FAMILIES
STATE OF PENNSYLVANIA
HARRISBURG, PENNSYLVANIA

Hillel Goelman
DEPARTMENT OF LANGUAGE EDUCATION
UNIVERSITY OF BRITISH COLUMBIA
VANCOUVER, BRITISH COLUMBIA
CANADA

Carollee Howes
GRADUATE SCHOOL OF EDUCATION
UNIVERSITY OF CALIFORNIA AT LOS ANGELES
LOS ANGELES, CALIFORNIA

Susan Kontos
DEPARTMENT OF CHILD DEVELOPMENT AND FAMILY STUDIES
PURDUE UNIVERSITY
WEST LAFAYETTE, INDIANA

Kathleen McCartney
DEPARTMENT OF PSYCHOLOGY
UNIVERSITY OF NEW HAMPSHIRE
DURHAM, NEW HAMPSHIRE

Alan R. Pence
SCHOOL OF CHILD CARE
UNIVERSITY OF VICTORIA
VICTORIA, BRITISH COLUMBIA
CANADA

Deborah A. Phillips
DEPARTMENT OF PSYCHOLOGY
UNIVERSITY OF VIRGINIA
CHARLOTTESVILLE, VIRGINIA

Sandra Scarr
DEPARTMENT OF PSYCHOLOGY
UNIVERSITY OF VIRGINIA
CHARLOTTESVILLE, VIRGINIA

Information About NAEYC

NAEYC is...

...a membership supported organization of people committed to fostering the growth and development of children from birth through age 8. Membership is open to all who share a desire to serve and act on behalf of the needs of and rights of young children.

NAEYC provides...

...educational services and resources to adults who work with and for children, including
- **Young Children,** *the* Journal for early childhood educators
- **Books, posters,** and **brochures** to expand your knowledge and commitment to young children, with topics including infants, curriculum, research, discipline, teacher education, and parent involvement
- An **Annual Conference** that brings people from all over the country to share their expertise and advocate on behalf of children and families
- **Week of the Young Child** celebrations sponsored by NAEYC Affiliate Groups across the country to call public attention to the needs and rights of children and families
- **Insurance plans** for individuals and programs
- **Public policy information** for informed advocacy efforts at all levels of government
- The **National Academy of Early Childhood Programs,** a voluntary accreditation system for high quality programs for young children
- **Child Care Information Service,** a computer-based, centralized source of information sharing, distribution, and collaboration.

For free information about membership, publications, or other NAEYC services...

...call NAEYC at 202-232-8777 or 800-424-2460 or write to NAEYC, 1834 Connecticut Ave., N.W., Washington, DC 20009-5786.